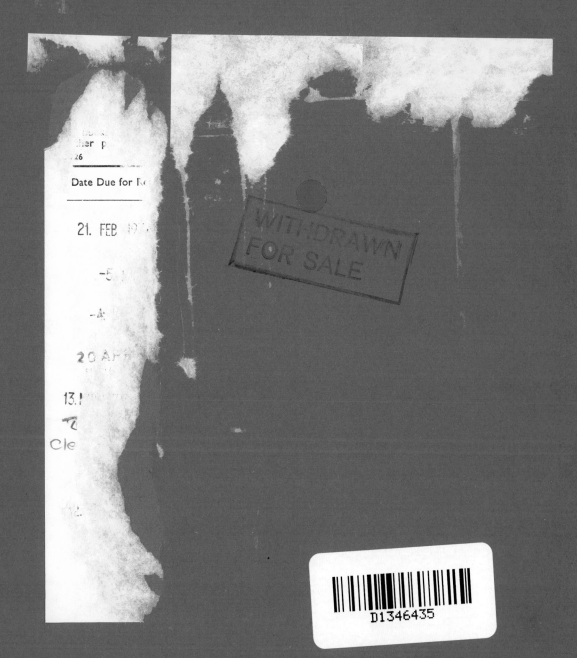

Encyclopaedia
of Planning

Graham Ashworth

Encyclopædia of Planning

With a preface by The Reverend The Lord Sandford
Parliamentary Under-Secretary of State, Department of the Environment

Barrie & Jenkins
London

Thanks are due to the following for permission to reproduce illustrations:

Airofilms Ltd (Nos 35 & 37) Airviews (Manchester) Ltd (No 2) Bedfordshire County Council (No 16) *Blackpool Gazette & Herald* (No 6) British Travel Association (No 9) Cement & Concrete Association (Nos 12 & 22) Civic Trust for the North West (Nos 18, 19, 48 & 49) Crawley Development Corporation (Nos 32 & 39) Derbyshire Councy Council (Nos 10 & 11) Dienst Van Stadsont Wirreling de Gemeente, Rotterdam (Nos 45 & 46) Forestry Commission (No 20) Great London Council (Nos 26 & 44) *The Guardian* (No 40) H.M.S.O. (Nos 17 & 36) Jill Krementz (No 31) Lancashire County Planning Dept. (No 15) Liverpool Record Office (No 34) Mack of Manchester Ltd (No 56) *Manchester Evening News* (No 23) Lotte Meitner-Graf (No 21) Ministry of Transport (Nos 53 & 54) National Trust (Nos 4 & 5) National Trust for Scotland (Nos 41 & 42) Ramsay & Muspratt, Oxford (No 50) Gordon Sommers (Nos 24 & 25) Taylor Woodrow Ltd (Nos 7 & 8) Unilever Research Laboratory (No 38)

First published in 1973 by
Barrie & Jenkins Limited
London.

Designed by Michael R. Carter.

Printed and bound in England by
Butler & Tanner Ltd,
Frome, Somerset.

ISBN 0 214 65079 0

Contents

Preface

by The Reverend The Lord Sandford Parliamentary Under-Secretary of State, Department of the Environment.

Graham Ashworth has provided us with this at a most timely moment.

1970 saw the birth of the British Department of the Environment—the first in the world.

1972 saw the United Nations Conference on the Environment at Stockholm—the first in history.

Never before has so much been done to repair the ravages left by the Industrial Revolution in our own land.

Never before have so many people been taking such a keen interest in the environment. More and more are becoming involved in seeking solutions. Those engaged professionally in doing so, and students, will find this book invaluable, but it is a book for the layman too.

Now that he has seen something of what can be done in managing and improving the environment, Mr 'Everyman' would like to see more being done, and he would like to have a larger say in deciding how it is done.

To amateur and professional alike this book provides an admirable guide.

Introduction

This book is about the planning of our physical environment.

To those constantly engaged in town and country planning in Britain it is a source of some surprise that people from all over the world should visit us to learn more of our system. Yet they do, and it is probably true that many foreigners are better informed about our system than most Britons. This book is an inadequate attempt to rectify that ignorance or confusion.

Confusion is probably a better word because planning is a misleadingly simple-sounding idea. We all plan. If not our families, then our businesses or our gardens. Or, at the very least, millions plan their holidays. Having an objective (or several) and then ordering time and talents towards those objectives is clearly a sound idea and when applied to a home or small business it remains simple. With the planning of a large business, or a town, however, it becomes involved; and the ordering of resources and skills in a city, region or whole country is almost infinitely complex.

Complexity always produces new techniques of practice and description. An elite group emerges (whether it is in the world of nuclear physics, aerospace, or Theology) speaking a language which is usually difficult for the rest of us to grasp, and at times wholly unintelligible. The scientist has his jargon: so does the planner. But there is one difference. The scientific pursuit does not require for its success, the understanding and acceptance by the general public whereas planning, if it is to succeed, must be accepted by those for whom the planning is done; at least in the modern sense of the word.

Of course the planning of towns has been going on for 10,000 years and this book tries to deal with some of the more significant people and events in that history. But it is only during the last 150 years and with the population and industrial growth of those years that the ordering of society as a whole and the management of land resources have become universally applicable. Not applied universally though, for many countries have not yet even covertly accepted the idea of planning with the control and restriction of individual liberty that are its corollaries. Even in Britain the idea of a National Physical Plan is eschewed, though partly achieved as each of the parts of Britain has a plan. If all these plans are added up together make a sort of National Plan. But a genuine National Plan would be much better and more than just the sum of a hundred parts. But planning is still feared, perhaps rightly, as the most obvious way in which the State or Bureaucracy may take over our lives. It's not that the fear is unfounded; just unfortunate. For the takeover should not be feared but accepted as inevitable with society becoming so complex.

Dissatisfaction with planners and their achievements, though, is no excuse for dismissing the idea of planning itself. It simply means that a lot more people must be willing to inform themselves about plans and surveys, about green belts and white land, about comprehensive development and listed buildings. It is my hope that this book may help.

Being a passionate believer in the idea of planning and so closely involved in my day-to-day life with its advocacy, it has been hard to keep this work factual and free of opinion; but I have tried. In any case some items are concerned with people and places whose part in the development of planning are unchallengeable. Their inclusion in this work is suggested by the part they have played in the evolution of the idea of town planning.

A work of this sort is inevitably indebted to many, including some published, sources. Among the books to which I am obviously indebted are: *Town and Country Planning in England,* by J. B. Cullingworth, (Allen & Unwin). *An Outline of Planning Law,* by Desmond Heap (Sweet & Maxwell). Latterly *Environment—a notebook* by Peter Cresswell (John Murray) was most useful as a check against my own work. Had it appeared sooner I might have despaired of the need to continue, though I believe the two books are complementary rather than repetitious.

Even though the book is arranged alphabetically there is an index to those persons and places that do not have an entry of their own but are mentioned in other entries.

It is impossible to list all those to whom I am indebted but some must be mentioned. Firstly to my collaborator, Ian Christie. He has worked tirelessly with me in preparing and writing many entries as well as assembling the photographs and drawings. At the outset Dennis Sharp was closely involved in the preparation of the list of entries and in drafting some. But at the end both the selection and responsibility for error are mine. Kathleen Henderson, my secretary, has patiently typed and retyped so much of the work it is impossible to overstate my indebtedness. My publishers have been pillars of patience. Finally, my thanks to my wife whose gentle reminders have helped me to complete the work.

Graham Ashworth

ABERCROMBIE, Sir Leslie Patrick, 1874–1957

Distinguished architect, town-planner, teacher and writer. Educated at Uppingham. He became an articled pupil to a firm of Manchester architects.

In 1913 he won a competition for the re-planning of Dublin. From 1915–35 he was Professor of Civic Design at Liverpool University and while there founded *The Town Planning Review*. Later in conjunction with J. H. Forshaw he prepared the *County of London Plan 1943*, for the London County Council. In 1944 he published his *Greater London Plan*. He also prepared numerous other plans for towns and cities throughout Britain as well as in Hong Kong and Cyprus.

A man of great distinction in his profession, Abercrombie served as President of the Town Planning Institute (1925–6) and was the first President of the International Union of Architects. He received many honours including the R.I.B.A. (q.v.) Royal Gold Medal in 1946; the Gold Medal of the American Institute of Architects, 1949.

He was knighted in 1946.

ADSHEAD, Stanley Davenport, 1868–1946

Architect, planner, writer and teacher who is perhaps best remembered as the first holder of the Lever Chair of Civic Design in Britain's first university town planning department at Liverpool University.

Son of a painter and Manchester Academician, Adshead spent the early years of his career working in the offices of various architects where he developed the fine talent for perspective drawing that enabled him to exhibit frequently in the Royal Academy and earned him a reputation as one of the best draughtsmen of his day. His time at Liverpool was not long. Following W. H. Lever's endowment of a Chair of Civic Design, he was invited by his friend Charles Reilly (q.v.), then professor of architecture, to be the first lecturer (1909) and, subsequently (1912), professor in the new department. He left in 1914 to become first professor of town planning at London University. But during those five years, by his teaching skills, his editorship (with Patrick Abercrombie (q.v.)) of the department's journal, *The Town Planning Review*, which he had helped found, and as an established and reputed draughtsman, he became a leading authority on design matters and obtained for his department an influence that was not confined either to Liverpool or to Britain.

On leaving Liverpool, Adshead continued in the partnership that involved him in many local authority housing schemes and the creation of the model village of Dormanstown near Middlesbrough for the employees of Dorman, Long & Co. Between 1911 and about 1931 he was responsible for the development of the Duchy of Cornwall Estate at Kennington, London. He was consultant to Norwich and Brighton Councils and throughout his career, in association with others, prepared a number of advisory reports on the South Teeside region, the Thames Valley, Scarborough, Essex, Teignmouth, York and other places. He was a founder member and President (1918–19) of the Town Planning Institute (q.v.), Vice-President of the Royal Institute of British Architects (q.v.) (1919–22), and a member of the Royal Fine Art Commission (q.v.) (1927–1934). He retired from London University in 1935.

Apart from various reports, his published books were:

Town Planning and Town Development (1923).

A New England: Planning for the Future (1941).

New Towns for Old (Design for Britain, Series 2, 1943).

ADVERTISEMENT CONTROL

With a few minor exceptions (e.g. within a building, on a moving vehicle, or as part of a building's fabric) the display of advertisements is controlled in this country by having established the principle in the Planning Acts, that they constitute 'development' (q.v.) and, as such, require planning permission. But in order to prevent the local planning authority (q.v.) being inundated with applications various administrative procedures have been established.

Provided they fall within the descriptions and measurements set out in the Advertisement Regulations 1969, advertisements may be deemed to have planning permission. Then, like certain other activities, they are permitted development (q.v.). If for any reason the local authority subsequently feels that the advertisement has a detrimental effect on amenity or is a hazard it may serve a 'Discontinuance Order' (q.v.).

If advertisements are to be larger than the dimensions laid down for deemed planning consent then Express Consent must be sought. If it is granted, a time limit of five years is normally imposed. There is a right of appeal against refusal of consent or imposed conditions.

All advertisements must comply with the conditions in the Regulations and so must be kept clean, tidy and safe and must not obscure traffic signs. Local planning authorities can keep an area almost free of advertisements by declaring it an Area of Special Control (q.v.).

FURTHER READING
Ministry of Housing and Local Government. *Planning Control of Signs and Posters*. 1966.
Sulton, James (1965). *Signs in Action*.
Adams, J. W. R. (1965). *Posters Look to the Future*.

AMENITY SOCIETIES

The first known amenity society, the Sidmouth Improvement Committee (now the Sid Vale Association), was formed in 1864 'for the purpose of proposing plans for the general improvement of the place . . . and also for securing to the public the existing walks on the cliffs and Salcombe Hill'.

Since then the number has grown, most significantly since 1957 following the formation of the Civic Trust (q.v.) which has fostered the formation of such societies. In 1970 there were over 800 societies registered with the Trust which, through its regional counterparts seeks to service the societies with advice and information.

The Trust also has a model constitution on which local societies may base their own. In most cases the society has a Chairman, Secretary, Treasurer and executive committee, elected annually at the Annual General Meeting. Often there are sub-committees for various aspects of the society's work, which consists of concerning itself with all manner of environmental matters, broadly similar, but at a local level, to those of the Civic Trust.

FURTHER READING
Civic Trust. *The Civic Society Movement*.
Civic Trust. *The Democratic Voice*. Reprint from Official Architecture and Planning. Vol. 31. Sept. 1968.
Percival, A. *Local Amenity Societies and Local Government*.
Percival, A. *The Organisation of an Amenity Society*.
All published by the Civic Trust.

ANCIENT MONUMENTS

An Ancient Monument may be an ancient building, a structure or earthwork or even a cave. It is scheduled by the Department of the Environment (Minister of Housing and Construction) and may be owned by a Local Authority or the Government, or be in their guardianship. In practice such ownership is the best, for it ensures a better measure of protection than those in private ownership obtain.

There are 12,000 scheduled ancient monuments and anyone may suggest additions to the schedule by writing to the Chief Inspector of Ancient Monuments who is responsible for administering the Ancient Monuments Acts under which the scheduling is authorised.

A scheduled monument is protected against demolition or alteration without the Minister's consent and any offence is punishable by fines

2

or even imprisonment. Detection of offences (deliberate or accidental) is difficult, and even when discovered an offence may be leniently treated by the courts.

Advice is given to the Minister by the Royal Commissions on Historic Monuments for England and there are equivalents in Scotland and Wales. Their staffs prepare detailed surveys and inventories.

FURTHER READING
Council for British Archaeology. *Memorandum on the Ancient Monuments Acts.*
Cambridgeshire and Isle of Ely Council. *A Guide to Historic Buildings Law* (1967).

A.P.R.R. (*see* Association for Planning and Regional Reconstruction).

ARCHITECTS ADVISORY PANELS
In many parts of the U.K. Development Control powers have been delegated (under the 1962 Town and Country Planning Act) to small District Councils (q.v.). These are often inadequately advised professionally and in some areas such councils have been encouraged to seek the advice of a panel of architects drawn from the local branch or society. This panel comments on the aesthetic aspects of any proposed development and advises the local council, which is free to ignore such advice.

To try to co-ordinate the activities of such panels and secure some form of overall national policy, an ad hoc committee (the Central Committee of Architects Advisory Panels) has been formed with a part-time secretariat to serve it.

ADDRESS
Central Committee of Architects Advisory Panels, 4, Hobart Place, London S.W.1.

AREA PLANNING OFFICER
In most county planning authorities, where the geographical area covered may be considerable, area planning offices are established to deal with parts of the county. Each office has an area planning officer in charge and his role is largely limited to development control functions. His advice is given to both the delegated planning authority (a district council (q.v.)) and the county planning authority. Where the delegated planning authority rejects the advice of the area planning officer on a particular planning application it is usually referred to the county planning authority, although systems of delegation differ.

A further role, though less frequent, is involvement in the preparation of development plans for towns and villages: this is normally done in association with the headquarters staff of the planning authority.

FURTHER READING
Cullingworth, J. B. (3rd Ed. 1970). *Town and Country Planning in England and Wales.*

AREAS OF OUTSTANDING NATURAL BEAUTY
As with National Parks (q.v.), these areas are defined by the Countryside Commission (q.v.) (formerly the National Parks Commission). The land in them remains in private ownership, but agreements or orders to secure additional public access may be made by the local authorities. Steps are taken to preserve and enhance the natural beauty of the landscape by high standards of development control, and by positive measures attracting grants (q.v.), such as tree planting and preservation, removal of eyesores and improvements of derelict land. Some 3,000 square miles in 20 areas had been designated as areas of outstanding natural beauty in 1966.

FURTHER READING
Ministry of Housing and Local Government (1970). *Development Plans.*

AREAS OF SPECIAL CONTROL (*see* Advertisement Control).
These may be designated by a Local Planning Authority (q.v.) as a means of controlling the display of advertisements. Normally advertise-

3

ments are treated as 'development' (q.v.) within the Town and Country Planning Acts and as such come under the requirements of development control. In an Area of Special Control, where it is usual for no advertisements to be allowed, those that are permitted are agreed exceptions to the rule.

ARTICLE 4 DIRECTION
Under the General Development Order 1963 (q.v.) certain activities are listed as not requiring planning permission. Gates, fences, painting and extensions to houses (below a certain size) are in this category. But a Planning Authority may make an Article 4 direction bringing such an activity back under development control. The Minister has to approve the direction and has to be convinced that there are special circumstances that justify it.

FURTHER READING
Heap, Desmond (5th Ed. 1969). *An Outline of Planning Law.*

ASSISTED AREAS
Parts of the country where special measures are seen to be necessary to encourage the growth and proper distribution of industry. Often such areas have high and persistent unemployment, or it is likely to occur.

In these areas Central Government (q.v.) through the Department of Trade and Industry can offer a number of different inducements to industrialists to settle or expand. The assisted areas have three classifications: Special Development Areas, Development Areas, and Intermediate Areas. The differences between them are principally in the level of assistance offered.

Broadly, the Department of Trade and Industry can build factories for leasing at favourable rents, or sale, or deferred terms; make a capital grant towards the building costs of an industrialist's own factory or for unusual initial expenses resulting solely from his choice of an assisted area; make grants (20% in Development Areas, $22\frac{1}{2}\%$ in Special Develop-

ment Areas) on plant and machinery; it can also make loans.

In addition, various government departments can make higher grants (q.v.) to local authorities for housing rehabilitation, clearing derelict land (q.v.) or neglected sites and for improving basic services, in Assisted Areas (e.g. for derelict land clearance the grant is 85% in Development Areas, 75% in Intermediate Areas as against 50% elsewhere).

Intermediate Areas are those parts of the country which, though not so impoverished as Development Areas, have a sufficiently slow rate of economic growth to cause concern. In 1969 the Hunt Committee reported on these areas. Although finding it difficult to identify a clear-cut category of intermediate area they felt that North West Yorkshire and Humberside stood in need of new impetus and special assistance and recommended more limited assistance to the Notts–Derbyshire coalfield and North Staffordshire.

Although rejecting most of the Report the Government did recognise the needs of some areas and defined them as intermediate areas, including North East Lancashire, the Yorkshire coalfield, South East Wales, Plymouth and Leith. Subsequently, areas have been altered or extended, including the declaration of the whole of the North West Region (q.v.) as an Intermediate Area.

FURTHER READING
Cullingworth, J. B. (3rd Ed. 1970). *Town and Country Planning in England and Wales.*

ASSOCIATION FOR PLANNING AND REGIONAL RECONSTRUCTION (A.P.R.R.)
The Association consisted of a group of people from many professions concerned with the fact that physical planning should be based on adequate preliminary survey work and that plans should result from a composite team of experts and not from a 'master-planner'. The Association served as a centre for matters concerning town planning and produced broadsheets and reports covering a wide range of planning subjects. In 1945 the Association

launched a series of publications called *Survey Before Plan*, to bridge the gap between the interested general public and the professionals.

FURTHER READING
Edited by A.P.R.R. *Town and Country Planning Textbook* issued in 1950.

B

BACON, Edmund Norwood 1910–

American architect, planner and author under whose leadership the renowned redevelopment and conservation of Philadelphia (q.v.) have been taking place continuously since 1949.

Bacon's other notable work is his book *Design of Cities* (1967), a detailed and illustrated exploration of urban spatial arrangements throughout history from which certain basic design principles are drawn.

Bacon received his architectural training at Cornell University and took his first job as architect designer in Shanghai. He entered private practice in 1935, was for two years city planner at Flint, Michigan (1937–9) and then became Director of the Philadelphia Housing Association (1940–43). He has worked with the Philadelphia City Planning Commission since 1946, becoming its Executive Director in 1949.

FURTHER READING
Johnson-Marshall, Percy (1966). *Rebuilding Cities.*

BARLOW REPORT: 1940

The report of a Royal Commission set up 'to inquire into the causes which have influenced the present geographical distribution of the industrial population of Great Britain and the probable direction of any change in that distribution in future, to consider what social, economic or strategic disadvantages arise from the concentration of industries or of the industrial population in large towns or in particular areas of the country; and to report what remedial measures if any should be taken in the national interest.'

The Report of the Commission was published in January 1940. It was a majority report with a note of reservation by three members. Three more (including Patrick Abercrombie) felt unable to sign at all. But the differences were more concerned with administration and machinery than as a result of any fundamental disagreement. Indeed there was a unanimous condemnation of the existing situation and the weakness of the policy and machinery for coping with it. It was clearly seen by all the commission members that government should play a far more active remedial role, that some control should be exercised over London and the Home Counties, that industry should be dispersed from the urban concentrations and that unemployment and economic depression should be anticipated by a proper investment programme.

The conclusions of the Commission and the need for munitions for the Second World War (which allowed new factories to be sited in areas of unemployment etc.) combined together to make the idea of town and country planning acceptable, at least in the matter of industrial location.

FURTHER READING
Cullingworth, J. B. (3rd ed. 1970). *Town Planning in England and Wales.*

BASTIDE TOWNS

Towns of the thirteenth and fourteenth centuries, mostly in France, that displayed a return from medieval irregularity to the formal planing of the Roman era.

The name 'Bastide' is closely related to bastille (fortress) and the towns were generally small, varied in form to suit local conditions and enclosed by a protective wall/ditch, as in the cases of Cadillac and Montpazier. They were easily recognised by the rectilinear street pattern that they embodied with right-angled crossed streets and a spacious central market square watched over by town hall and church.

There were some English 'bastide' towns quite a bit later, but their more irregular organic arrangements suggest that urbanism in medieval England was rather poor.

FURTHER READING
Hiorns, Frederick R. (1956). *Town Building in History.*

BATH
The development of Bath from a small medieval walled city to Britain's largest and most fashionable spa is the most outstanding example of large-scale eighteenth century town planning in the country and one of the finest in the world.

The extension took place in three distinct phases: the early sequence of enclosed interrelated architectural spaces (1728–54), leading from Queen Square through Gay Street to The Circus, in which John Wood the elder gave an entirely new metropolitan scale to the simple terrace house by transforming it into one element within a larger monumental entity; the more open and curvilinear development to the north west (1767–75) where John Wood the younger and John Palmer brought parkland and trees into integral relationship with Royal and Lansdown Crescents; and the unfinished Bathwick 'new town' (1788–93), over Pulteney Bridge, where Palmer and Thomas Baldwin reverted to a more formal and geometrical layout but adopted a Baroque scale and massiveness absent from the first phase.

It is scarcely possible to exaggerate Bath's influence on subsequent English townscapes (q.v.). An urban style had been created, compact yet spacious, formal and imposing yet human in scale, that was to appear again not only at the spas and resorts of Brighton, Bristol, Buxton, Cheltenham and Weymouth, but also at Edinburgh (q.v.) and in John Nash's scheme linking St James's Park to Regent's Park in London. [*see also* Four Town Reports]

FURTHER READING
Colin Buchanan and Partners. *Bath: A Study in Conservation* (1968).
Johns, Ewart (1965). *British Townscapes.*
Bell, Colin and Rose (1969) *City Fathers.*

BEDFORD PARK
The first garden suburb (1876–81). It was developed in and around the former gardens and orchard of Bedford House near Turnham Green Station, Chiswick, and intended primarily for 'artistic people of moderate income'. The developer, Jonathan Carr, was an acquaintance of William Morris.

Most of the houses were semi-detached and designed by Norman Shaw in the friendly, trim and exuberant 'Queen Anne revival' style with its bright red brick, white painted woodwork, and abundance of gables and dormers. The wide streets, loosely arranged, were planted with limes, poplars and willows and the building line was varied to preserve the maximum number of existing trees and create interesting street pictures.

It was the emphasis on trees, verdure and a picturesque informality which distinguished Bedford Park from earlier suburbs with their regimented street patterns, and which brought it wide publicity through American, German and English publications. The arcadian imagery had been provided and was to be adopted, adapted and diluted in a multitude of subsequent suburban developments.

FURTHER READING
Creese, Walter, J. (1966). *The Search for Environment (The Garden City Before and After)*
Burke, G. (1971). *Towns in the Making.*

BENEFICIAL USE
A phrase that occurs frequently in planning affairs and means, bluntly, what it says. But interpretations vary and what one party to a dispute may accept as beneficial use may be rejected by the other.

Questions of beneficial use arise when a landowner, having been refused planning consent or had swingeing conditions imposed, or received a revocation of planning permission or a discontinuance order (q.v.), or experienced planning blight (q.v.), feels he can no longer obtain 'beneficial use' out of his land and so serves a purchase notice (q.v.) on the Local Planning Authority.

FURTHER READING
Cullingworth, J. B. (3rd Ed. 1970). *Town and Country Planning in England and Wales.*

BETTERMENT
The increased value of a piece of land as a result of some planning proposal being given permission.

Betterment is the logical balance to compensation (q.v.) paid to a landowner when his property is adversely affected. But it has always proved difficult to collect and, despite the recommendations of the Uthwatt Committee (q.v.), the provisions of the 1947 Act and the attempts of the Land Commission (q.v.), it is not collected today.

FURTHER READING
Cullingworth, J. B. (3rd Ed. 1970). *Town and Country Planning in England and Wales.*

BIRKENHEAD PARK (*see* Paxton, Joseph).

BLIGHT
The word used to describe the effect of long-term planning proposals on the value of property affected by those proposals. As a result of blight a landowner may find himself unable to sell his property at all or only at a depreciated price, even though the proposals may not be implemented for many years.

There is no compensation (q.v.) for blight, although an owner can serve a purchase notice (q.v.) on the local planning authority (q.v.) if he can show that his property is no longer capable of reasonably beneficial use (q.v.). It is slightly easier to get the purchase notice accepted if the property is actually going to be acquired in less than fifteen years. But many

properties not actually needed for the proposed development (q.v.) (road, school, etc.) are none-the-less affected and their value depreciated. This often results in hardship despite the Department of the Environment asking Local Authorities to treat such areas sympathetically.

It may reasonably be said that Blight is one of two main reasons for planning (q.v.) being unpopular with the general public, the other being the delays often experienced in obtaining decisions.

FURTHER READING
Ministry of Housing and Local Government. Circulars 49/59, 15/69, 46/70.

BOROUGH COUNCIL (*see* Local Government).

BOULEVARD (Fr.)
A public avenue or street laid out with trees and belts of grass. Used originally to describe a decoratively laid out street on the site of old fortifications, e.g. some boulevards in Paris laid out by Hausmann (q.v.) follow the fortifications pattern. Now has a much wider meaning that includes any street laid out with lines of trees and green verges, e.g. The Mall, London; Lord Street Boulevard, Southport.

FURTHER READING
Gibberd, Frederick (3rd Ed. 1959). *Town Design.*
Hiorns, F. (1956). *Town Building in History.*

BOURNVILLE
A pioneering and influential experiment in community planning started in 1879 by George Cadbury for the workers at his factory resited five miles outside Birmingham.

Physically, Bournville is distinguished from all previous model villages except Port Sunlight (q.v.) by the liberal provision of open space and by its picturesque appearance. Although the first development followed the rectilinear bye law street pattern, later layouts

1. Bournville in 1898: Plan

were looser and more influenced by the contours of the site. Streets were wide and consciously curved and their margins were planted with exotic and flowering trees. Cadbury's stipulations that no building should occupy more than one quarter of its site and that one tenth of the estate, excluding roads and private gardens, should be given over to public open space and recreation grounds, ensured that verdure and horticulture were conspicuous and integral in all developments. Houses at a density of 7 or 8 to the acre were in pairs or groups and sited so as not to face each other directly. A variety of materials and textures were used to obtain interesting street pictures and a rustic character. The village eventually covered 842 acres.

Although Bournville can be considered to represent a culmination of the nineteenth century movement in housing and social reforms, it was not designed, like its predecessors at New Lanark. Saltaire (q.v.) Akroydon and elsewhere to house merely its industrialist's employees. Workers at the chocolate factory have numbered only about 50 per cent of the working population. It was intended to be an example of community planning with much wider implications for the housing problems of the major industrial cities. Certainly the health statistics which Cadbury liked to quote were impressive: children at Bournville were found to be several pounds heavier and several inches taller than their contemporaries in one area of Birmingham. The project was also financially successful with houses let at moderate rents yielding a return of 4 per cent on capital investment.

Together with a number of other experiments at the turn of the century, Bournville had a considerable influence on the writings and projects of Ebenezer Howard (q.v.) and, through him, on the content and aims of the first planning legislation.

FURTHER READING
Bell, Colin and Rose (1969). *City Fathers.*
Creese, W. J. (1966). *The search for Environment (The Garden City Before and After.)*
Ashworth, W. (1954). *The Genesis of Modern British Town Planning.*
Burke, G. (1971). *Towns in the Making.*

BRASILIA
The capital of Brazil and a completely new twentieth-century city which more than any other, apart from Chandigarh (q.v.), shows the influence of Le Corbusier's (q.v.) theories of city planning.

The competition-winning plan of Brasilia was designed by Lucio Costa and is of striking simplicity. Derived from a sketch on an envelope, it is shaped like an aeroplane, with the cathedral, opera house and a monumental complex of government buildings occupying the nose and residential apartment blocks occupying the wings. The main commercial and entertainment area is situated in the fuselage and centred around the multi-level bus terminal which marks its juncture with the expressway running down the middle of the wings. Two superblocks away from the expressway and parallel with it, is a linear pedestrian shopping way. There are no traffic intersections at all. On three sides the edge of the city centre is defined by a huge artificial

opposite
Bournville Today
2. View from the air
3. Part of the original estate.

8

lake. Most of the buildings to date have been designed by the leading modern architect of Brazil, Oscar Niemeyer.

There are essentially two attitudes towards Brasilia. To its critics it represents a synthesis of all that is most grandiose, autocratic and sterile in the architectural and planning theories of Le Corbusier. The buildings in the centre are admired for their simplicity of form, but they are admired as pieces of beautifully shaped sculpture, carefully related to each other but placed too far apart either to define space or to create the sense of enclosure that is associated with the traditional city. They are stunning to look at but uncomfortable and inconvenient to live with. In the view of its apologists, however, Brasilia represents a potent new urban aesthetic, in which buildings do not (and are not intended to) enclose or define space, but, rather, function as punctuation of continuous space. Costa himself has pointed out that the dense Brasilian cloud formations were considered as an integral part of the city's design, providing an ever-changing backcloth to the buildings and helping to tie them together.

It is also stressed that Brasilia was not intended to be a model for other cities. Like Chandigarh, it had a unique and symbolical role; situated on virgin land 1,000 kilometres from the Atlantic coast and replacing the sea-board capital of Rio de Janeiro, it was designed to open up and stimulate the development of Brazil's hiterto largely underdeveloped interior. The population in 1960 was 141,172.

FURTHER READING
Bacon, E. (1967). *Design of Cities.*
Evenson, Norma (1969). *Le Corbusier: the Machine and the Grand Design.*

BRIDLEWAYS (*see* Footpaths).

BUCHANAN, Sir Colin Douglas 1907–
Was born in India and educated at Berkham-stead School and what is now the Imperial College of Science and Technology, London University.

After a period as an assistant to a firm of town planning consultants in Essex he took up an appointment with the Civil Service as a Ministry of Transport Executive at Exeter.

During the Second World War he served in the Royal Engineers, rising to the rank of Lieutenant-Colonel.

After the war he joined the Ministry of Town and Country Planning and was involved with many public inquiries (q.v.) into many projects of national interest.

He is the author of *Mixed Blessing, A study of the Motor in Britain,* a book which eventually led him to be appointed by Ernest Marples, the then Conservative Minister of Transport, to make a study, 'of the long-term development of roads and traffic in urban areas' and 'the effect that it is likely to have on the cities of Britain'. In 1963 the H.M.S.O. report by Buchanan and his team of specialists, *Traffic in Towns,* appeared. It was an amazingly lucid and well designed publication aimed at pro-viding the Government with a policy document for use of motor vehicles in towns throughout the country. Buchanan, almost overnight, became a household word, praised by his colleagues and misunderstood by so many officials.

Since the appearance of his report Buchanan has become Professor of Transport at Imperial College and has carried out a number of important schemes for traffic reorganisation and environmental improvement. Major studies have included the future development of the cities of Bath (q.v.), Cardiff, Canterbury and Edinburgh (q.v.), the feasibility of large scale urban growth in the areas of Portsmouth and Southampton. Work overseas has included a development study for Kuwait, Arras in France, and studies in Nairobi. Created a Commander of the Order of the British Empire in 1964, Buchanan was awarded the Patrick Abercrombie (q.v.) award of the International Union of Architects in 1965. He is a Past President of the Royal Town Planning Institute (q.v.). In 1967 he was awarded the Gold Medal of the R.T.P.I. and is a Fellow of the Royal Society of Arts. He was knighted in 1972.

BUILDING PRESERVATION NOTICE
To secure the preservation of any building of architectural or historic interest and which

is not a listed building (q.v.), a local authority may make a Building Preservation Notice restricting the demolition, alteration or extension of the building. 'Building' includes structures and erections, thus a B.P.N. can be made not only in respect of buildings, but also in respect of such matters as ancient market crosses, village stocks, pumps, fountains, etc. It has the same effect on the building as if it were listed and applies for the six months during which time the Secretary of State for the Environment may be asked to consider listing it.

Carrying out unauthorised works to listed buildings or contravening a B.P.N. constitutes an indictable offence. In the Magistrate's Courts the maximum fine is £250 and/or three months' imprisonment. In higher courts there is no limit to the fine and in addition or as an alternative a sentence of twelve months' imprisonment may be given.

Wilful damage is also penalised. Anyone who causes or allows damage to a listed building is liable to a fine of £100 and required to take steps to prevent any further damage. Failure to do so is punishable at the rate of £20 per day for as long as the offence continues. Local Authorities may carry out first aid repairs to unoccupied listed buildings or those subject to a B.P.N. They may also compulsorily acquire such buildings that are not being properly preserved.

FURTHER READING
Cambridgeshire and Isle of Ely Council (2nd Ed. 1970). *A Guide to Historic Buildings Law.*

BY-PASS
A road which enables through traffic to avoid a locality through which it would otherwise have to pass.

C.B.A. (*see* Council for British Archaeology).

C.D.A. (*see* Comprehensive Development).

CENTRAL GOVERNMENT
The responsibility for economic and physical planning rests ultimately with Parliament and the government. Some departments of government are more concerned with it than others and the shape and quality of our environment rests primarily with three (allowing that the environment is also inevitably affected by economic planning which is the responsibility of the Treasury).

Foremost of the three is the Department of the Environment which is responsible for the full spectrum of functions that shape our surroundings. It covers all land use planning, the construction industry, housing and transport and is presided over by a Secretary of State,

with a seat in the Cabinet. He has three supporting Ministers:

The Minister for Local Government and Development (M.L.G.D.) whose responsibilities include regional land use planning; transport planning; local government; road passenger transport; water, sewerage and refuse disposal; countryside planning and conservation.

The Minister of Housing and Construction (M.H.C.) whose responsibilities include: housing programmes and finance; housing improvement; new towns (q.v.); building research; building government buildings; building regulations; the care of Royal Parks and Palaces and the conservation of Ancient Monuments (q.v.).

The Minister of Transport Industries who is responsible for ports; broad policy on nationalised transport (including railways and waterways); vehicle safety, licensing and freight haulage.

Of lesser importance but still affecting the shape of the environment are:

(i) The Department of Trade and Industry which is responsible for the location and planning of power stations, government policy on coal, gas, electricity and oil. It ultimately looks after airports and the location of industry and in this latter connection administers Industrial Development Certificates (q.v.) which are necessary for any new industrial building or extension above a certain size. The department also manages the financial incentives that can be offered to attract industry to Development Areas (q.v.).

(ii) The Ministry of Agriculture, which is consulted by local planning authorities when they consider applications to develop agricultural land. The shape of the countryside can be affected by the policies, grants and subsidies which it administers.

FURTHER READING

Central Office of Information (Annual). *Britain: An Official Handbook.*

Sharp, Evelyn (1969). *The Ministry of Housing and Local Government.*

CENTRAL RESERVATION

Strip of land (usually planted) between road carriageways on which traffic is moving in opposite directions.

CENTRE OF URBAN STUDIES

Established at University College, London, in 1958. The Centre has as its objects to contribute to the systematic knowledge of towns, in particular British towns; to study urban development, structure and society; and to link academic social research with social policy.

The Centre undertakes and assists a variety of relevant studies in this country and is in touch with research abroad.

Governed by a committee drawn from many disciplines including planning, architecture, statistics, sociology, law, public health, geography, etc.

The Centre publishes a series of studies on current town planning problems.

CHANDIGARH

Capital of the Punjab province of India, and the only realised plan of Le Corbusier (q.v.).

The original Master Plan by Albert Mayer was modified by Le Corbusier to become a regular grid of major roads for rapid transport surrounding residential superblocks or sections each based on the golden rectangle and measuring $800 \times 1,200$ metres. Each sector is served by internal distributor roads and bisected by a shopping street which itself bisects a linear strip of parkland containing pedestrian paths and schools. These strips extend through neighbouring sectors to form continuous corridors of open space throughout the city. A Capitol Complex containing sculpture and government buildings set amongst artificial earth mounds and lakes is sited at the north eastern edge of the city, the commercial district is placed near the centre and an industrial zone to one side. The measurement of 800 metres, which also occurs in the Capitol Complex, derives from Le Corbusier's patented Modulor system of proportioning and is also found in the layout of Paris which he admired. The whole plan represents a large scale application of the Radburn (q.v.) principle regularised by Le Corbusier's predilection for the rectilinear and the monumental. The population is planned to reach 500,000.

Chandigarh replaced the old capital of Lahore, which was ceded to Pakistan at the partition of India in 1947, and was thus not only required to fulfil the normal functions of a capital city but also to be a statement of national strength and the independence. 'Let this be a new town symbolical of the freedom of India, unfettered by the traditions of the past . . . an expression of the nation's faith in the future.' (President Nehru) Its symbolical power is widely recognised. The massive buildings by Le Corbusier in the Capitol Complex have a monumental strength and evocative plasticity of form which place them among the supreme, and supremely individual, achievements of twentieth-century architecture.

In functional terms, however, the city may be considered to illustrate a schematic and comprehensive application of Western planning concepts unconstrained and uninformed by any real appreciation of either the climate or the needs of an unmotorised, undeveloped nation. Although responsible for the Master Plan and adviser on all aspects of the development of Chandigarh, Le Corbusier devoted most of his energies to the design of the Capitol Complex, leaving much of the additional work to a group of designers including his cousin, Pierre Jeanneret, and two British architect members of the Congrès Internationaux d'Architecture Moderne (C.I.A.M.) (q.v.) Jane Drew and Maxwell Fry.

FURTHER READING
Evenson, Norma (1966). *Chandigarh*.
Evenson, Norma (1969). *Le Corbusier: the Machine and the Grand Design*.

CHESTER (*see* Four Towns Report).

CHICHESTER (*see* Four Towns Report).

C.I.A.M. (*see* Congrès Internationaux d'Architecture Moderne).

CIRCULARS
Periodic papers issued by the Department of the Environment which are written as guidance for local authorities, suggesting policies that might be pursued in respect of current legislation. In practice, for all their diplomatic phraseology, these circulars are instructions to the local authorities.

CIVIC AMENITIES ACT 1967
The Civic Amenities Bill was introduced into Parliament in July 1966, as a Private Member's measure, by Rt. Hon Duncan Sandys M.P., President of the Civic Trust. From its inception the Bill had the support of all parties in Parliament, Members on Government and Opposition benches in both Houses joined forces to improve it and the Bill received Royal Assent on 27 July 1967.

The Preamble to the Act reads as follows:

An Act to make further provision for the protection and improvement of buildings of architectural or historic interest and of the character of areas of such interest; for the preservation and planting of trees; and for the orderly disposal of disused vehicles and equipment and other rubbish.

Part 1 of the Act deals with the preservation of areas and buildings of architectural and historic interest. It makes provision, for the first time, for the protection of areas (as distinct from individual buildings) of cities, towns or villages. It also strengthens the law in relation to the preservation of individual buildings of architectural or historic interest.

Part II of the Act provides means for planting more trees with new development and makes tree preservation orders more effective.

Part III of the Act makes provision for the disposal of derelict motor cars and other bulky rubbish. It makes it an offence to abandon vehicles on the highway and places new duties on Local Authorities to provide proper facilities for the collection of old cars and other similar unwanted articles, thus making it easier for people to get rid of bulky rubbish.

Although the Act deals with three widely differing subjects, the link between them is that, in each case, it seeks to improve the appearance of town and countryside; by preserving and improving the appearance of historic towns; by planting more trees and by providing for the removal and disposal of old cars and other rubbish, which (being difficult to get rid of conveniently) so often disfigure the scene. Each part of the Act imposes new duties on Local Authorities and at the same time puts new responsibilities on individuals.

The Act applies to England, Wales and Scotland, but does not extend to Northern Ireland. Variations of the provisions applicable to Scotland are contained in the Act.

CIVIC CENTRE
The area in a town or city where the principal public buildings, e.g. town hall, municipal offices, public library, and other civic buildings are situated.

FURTHER READING
Johnson-Marshall, Percy (1966). *Rebuilding Cities*.

CIVIC TRUSTS

Founded in 1957 by the Rt Hon. Duncan Sandys (q.v.) the Civic Trust has as its basic purpose the promotion of better standards of planning and architecture, including the conservation of buildings or areas of architectural or historical importance.

It is a charity subscribed to by industry and commerce and is managed by a Board of Trustees and full-time Director and office staff. Individual membership is not considered, though there are some individual subscribers. Associate Civic Trusts now exist in the North West and North East of England and in Scotland and Wales. These are autonomous bodies, again being charities and each having its own Board of Trustees. The chairman of each Regional Trust is a trustee of the National Civic Trust. No other formal link exists, though informally there is close liaison. Each of the Associate Trusts has a full-time Director and staff.

Registered with the Trusts are local civic/amenity societies (q.v.) sometimes misleadingly called Trusts. These are constituted quite differently, being local and similar to many other societies, holding annual meetings and having executive committees. Anybody may join on payment of the membership fees and is entitled to vote etc. at general meetings.

ADDRESSES

Civic Trust, 17, Carlton House Terrace, London, S.W.1.

Civic Trust for the North East, 34/35 Saddler Street, Durham.

Civic Trust for the North West, 56, Oxford Street, Manchester.

Civic Trust for Wales, University of Wales, Inst. of Science and Technology, Greyfriars Road, Cardiff.

Scottish Civic Trust, 24, George Square, Glasgow, C.2.

CLEAN AIR

A term used to describe an atmosphere substantially free of smoke and other pollutants and embodied in the Clean Air Acts of 1956 and 1968. The 1956 Act enabled local councils to control smoke by designating areas as smokeless zones. Not all local authorities have used the legislation and substantial pollution still occurs in certain heavily industrialised areas, such as the Potteries.

Industry is not the only, nor indeed the main, source of pollution, domestic fires still contributing the majority of atmospheric pollution. Any noxious or offensive emission may be referred to the Public Health Inspector for enquiry.

FURTHER READING

Ministry of Housing and Local Government (1970). *Alkali Inspectorate. Annual Report.*

Reynolds, F. A. (1969). *A Critical Review of Current Clean Air Legislation.* Royal Society of Health Journal. Vol. 89. Nov.–Dec.

CLEARANCE AREAS

Areas where the local authority intends to demolish buildings, clear the site and build afresh. To achieve this they buy up property by agreement or, if necessary, by compulsory purchase. This concept differs from Comprehensive Development Areas (q.v.) where the area is to be developed and redeveloped as a whole. Clearance Areas can be developed piecemeal once the clearance has been achieved.

CLOVER LEAF

A two-level intersection between roads at right angles to each other which allows all vehicles to move freely whatever manoeuvre they are performing. No right turns are permitted (where traffic is driving on the left). The junction gets its name from the resulting plan shape.

FURTHER READING

Drake, James (1969). *Motorways.*

COASTLINE

Widespread interest in the coastlines of Western Europe has occurred only recently as the various pressures for its use (and misuse) have increased. It is now an oft-repeated subject for debate in planning circles and tighter control and acquisition by some 'national' body are

opposite
Coastline
4. Blackpool Sands, Devon
5. Helmsley, Norfolk

both advocated as means of securing its preservation.

In England and Wales the 2,600 miles of coastline have been under the protection of an advanced planning system for 20 years but in 1963 the Minister of Housing and Local Government decided that the problem merited special study and control. Maritime planning authorities were asked to make a special study of their coastal areas. In 1966 the Minister circularised local authorities urging the need for effective action to safeguard unspoilt stretches of coast. Within six months all the appropriate planning authorities were to submit clear statements of policy for their coastal areas.

In 1965 the National Trust launched 'Enterprise Neptune' to raise two million pounds and aimed to buy some 900 miles of coastline to protect it.

The effective management, control and in some cases recovery, of the 1,700 miles outside such ownership remains one of the major planning problems facing Britain today.

FURTHER READING
Steers, J. A. (4th Ed. 1969). *The Sea Coast.*
Cullingworth, J. B. (3rd Ed. 1970). *Town and Country Planning in England and Wales.*
Countryside Commission (1970). *Report on Coastline.*

'COFFIN'
The central strip of industrial England stretching from Brighton on the South Coast to Blackpool.

COMMON
Strictly a piece of land (not necessarily publicly owned) to which commoners (originally people of the district) have certain rights such as grazing cattle, cutting hay or bracken. Commons cannot be enclosed but as the need of commoners to have access for their livelihood has

6. Common Land: Wrea Green, Lancashire

diminished the commons have become open spaces with free public access. Confusion as to maintenance and use has grown over the years and the 1965 Commons Registration Act sought to clarify the position and utilize these spaces more sensibly. Two registers were thus established and completed in 1970, one for commons and one for town and village greens.

FURTHER READING
Christian, Garth. (1966). *Tomorrow's Country-side.*
Denman D. R. and others. *Commons and Village Greens.*
Ministry of Housing and Local Government Circulars 2/70 and 74/70.

COMMUNICATIONS
The network of canals, railways and roads that cover the country and the vessels or vehicles that use them. Not usually used in planning circles to describe telegraphy, radio or television.

COMMUNITY CENTRE
This can describe a number of buildings devoted to public use, e.g. library, meeting hall, shops, school, evening institute, situated in a town or village, or a single building used for community activities of all kinds on a housing estate. Unlike a Civic Centre (q.v.) it does not serve the whole town but only the immediate community needs.

COMPENSATION
The notion of the State or Local Authority paying money to a business or individual whose property is affected by planning proposals or public works.

Compensation—fair market value plus something for disturbances—is paid when a property is compulsorily acquired or part of it is acquired. In the latter case additional compensation is paid for loss of value of the rest (injurious affection).

In practice, where property is not actually affected and a loss in value occurs by virtue of an adjacent development (motorway or in-

dustrial estate) no compensation is paid—except rarely and after a great battle.

Equally rarely is compensation paid for planning Blight (q.v.) when the value of property is depreciated by some long-term planning proposals.

FURTHER READING
Heap, Desmond. (5th Ed. 1969). *An Outline of Planning Law.*
Lawrence, David M. (4th ed. 1969). *Compulsory Purchase and Compensation.*

COMPREHENSIVE DEVELOPMENT
The complete development or re-development of a sizeable area as a phased operation in accordance with a comprehensive plan for the whole area.

The idea of comprehensive development has become universally accepted for a number of reasons. With the great increase in motor traffic clearly many small individual developments would create impossible problems. Some form of collective servicing and parking access arrangements are essential. Similarly, standards of lighting, open space and fire resistance have all underlined the advantages of comprehensive development. Whilst there is a minimum amount of development that must take place so that any part of the overall scheme may function separately, it is the planning which must be comprehensive.

Comprehensive Development Area (C.D.A.) is an area defined by a local planning authority, within its development plan, for comprehensive development. In order to secure this comprehensive development the planning authority could use its powers of compulsory acquisition. To do this it has to designate the area as subject to Compulsory Acquisition by the making of a Compulsory Purchase Order (q.v.). This is the subject of a Public Inquiry and requires the confirmation of the Secretary of State for the Environment.

FURTHER READING
Ministry of Housing and Local Government. *Development Plans.* (1970).
Cullingworth, J. B. (3rd Ed. 1970). *Town and Country Planning in England and Wales.*

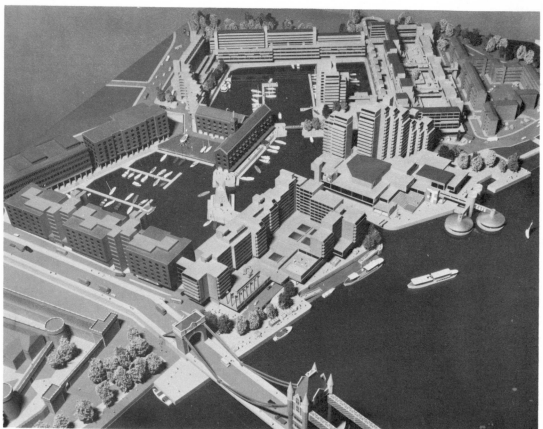

COMPULSORY PURCHASE AND COMPULSORY PURCHASE ORDER

The Town and Country Planning Act 1962 provides for land to be designated as being subject to compulsory purchase.

Compulsory purchase, falls into three categories.

It can apply to land

(i) for the purposes of any of the functions of the acquiring authority (Local council, Statutory Undertaker (q.v.), or Minister).

(ii) comprised in or adjacent to an area of comprehensive development.

(iii) which ought in the opinion of the local planning authority (q.v.) to be acquired to secure its use in the manner proposed by the development plan.

In all cases a compulsory purchase order (C.P.O.) in accordance with the Acquisition of Land (Authorisation Procedure) Act 1946, is made by the Local Planning Authority (q.v.) and confirmed by the Minister (after a public inquiry, where there are objections).

FURTHER READING
Heap, Desmond (Editor). *Encyclopaedia of Compulsory Purchase.*

CONGRES INTERNATIONAUX D'ARCHITECTURE MODERNE [C.I.A.M.]

This was set up at Chateau de la Sarraz, Switzerland, in June 1928.

Members of the congress have included such distinguished architect/planners as Le Corbusier, Walter Gropius, Cor van Eesteren, J. Luis Sert, etc.

In 1933, at the 4th C.I.A.M. Congress, the *Charte d'Athènes* was agreed and the four main functions of urban planning stated: living, working, recreation and communication (circulation).

Further meetings were held through to the end of the 50's but at length the whole idea collapsed. Nevertheless in two major periods (1930–4 and 1950–55) C.I.A.M. was the

opposite
Comprehensive Development
7. St. Catherine's Docks Today
8. Model of Taylor Woodrow's planned development for St. Catherine's Docks

channel through which the concepts of modern town planning and architecture came to be understood in the wider world. It may be that this in itself is a greater achievement than any particular subject discussed and documented by C.I.A.M.

FURTHER READING
Giedion, S. (1951). *A Decade of New Architecture*. Zurich.

CONSERVATION

A term used interchangeably with preservation but having the rather more positive connotation of adaptation of parts of a building (or countryside) whilst retaining the essential spirit of the original.

FURTHER READING
Ministry of Housing and Local Government. Circulars 53/67 and 61/68.
Nicholson, Max (1969). *The Environmental Revolution*.

CONSERVATION AREA

An area containing a group of buildings of special architectural or historical significance, which a Local Authority may designate under the Civic Amenities Act 1967 (q.v.). Such designation does not preclude the re-development of buildings within it but it does ensure a proper consideration of the desirability, form and material of any proposed development.

FURTHER READING
Civic Trust (1969). *Conservation Areas, A Selected Bibliography 1967–69.*
Civic Trust. *Progress in Creating Conservation Areas.* Nos. 1–16. Now called *Conservation Progress.*
Ward, Pamela (1968). *Conservation and Development. York Conference on Historic Town and Cities.*
Worskett, Roy (1969). *The Character of Towns.*

CONURBATION

A word first used by Patrick Geddes (q.v.) to describe a continuously built up area. Since

19

9. Conservation Area: Stamford, Lincolnshire

that time it has often been misused but in correct current usage still has the same meaning. Merseyside, Greater Manchester and the unbroken development around Birmingham and London are all conurbations.

FURTHER READING
Self, Peter (2nd Ed. 1961). *Cities in Flood.*
Storm, Michael (1965). *Urban Growth in Britain.*

LE CORBUSIER 1887–1965
Pseudonym adopted by the French architect, planner and polemicist Charles-Edouard Jeanneret who, by his visionary city planning schemes, has probably had a more profound influence on modern architecture and town design than any other individual.

Le Corbusier first formulated his concept of a city designed entirely to meet twentieth century needs in his proposal for an imaginary 'City for Three Million People' (1922). Other later schemes contained refinements and modifications to meet particular circumstances, but all of them were to a large extent variations on the essential imagery of this early proposal in which Le Corbusier envisaged tall freestanding skyscrapers and slab apartment blocks, each of uniform shape, height and appearance, placed far apart among trees in large parklike open spaces within a rigidly rectilinear framework of broad multi-level highways. Everywhere in buildings and roads, the straight line, right angle and complete standardisation were to manifest man's total mastery of his environment and would be set off by quantities of open space, greenery, fresh air and sunlight never obtainable in a high density development before. The plan was thus an entirely original combination of two previously separate and already influential strands in planning thought: the garden city idea with its emphasis on open space and a loosening of the urban fabric on the one hand, and the ideas of Sant'Elia (q.v.)

20

Tony Garnier (q.v.) and the Futurists with their enthusiasm for speed, mechanisation and technology on the other.

It was a fusion that immediately captured the imagination of the architectural and planning community and was to exert an enduring influence in universities and training schools for the next thirty years. One has only to look at Le Corbusier's sketches to realise the extent of the inspiration that has been drawn from them, consciously and unconsciously throughout the world.

Although Le Corbusier later prepared planning schemes for numerous places, among them Paris, Antwerp, Montevideo, Sao Paulo, Rio de Janeiro, Buenos Aires, Algiers, Saint Dié and Chandigarh (q.v.), only the last was ever fully executed. He was, however, able to illustrate some of his ideas on a smaller scale at Nemours in Algeria, where a geometrical arrangement of apartment blocks helped to establish the fashion for high rise (q.v.) slabs, and at Marseilles where his philosophy of 'vertical living' received its fullest expression in the famous and monumental Unité d'Habitation (originally conceived as one of a number of blocks) housing 1,600 people and containing internal shopping streets and community facilities. This and similar blocks at Nantes, Berlin and Briey-la-Forêt were widely imitated. In England their influence is most apparent at Roehampton (q.v.).

Le Corbusier was born in Switzerland, trained in Vienna, Paris and Berlin (under Peter Behrens) and entered private practice in 1922. He was a founder member of the C.I.A.M. (q.v.) and its manifesto of 1933, the Athens Charter, was largely his work. He was awarded the Gold Medal of the Royal Institute of British Architects (q.v.) in 1953. His principal works on planning were:

Towards a New Architecture (1923).
The City of the Future (1924).
Le Corbusier and Pierre Jeanneret, 1910–29 (1947).
When the Cathedrals Were White (1947).
New World of Space (1948).
Concerning Town Planning (1949).
The Marseilles Block (1953).

Complete Architectural Works, 1910–65 (1964/5).

FURTHER READING
Evanson, Norma. Le Corbusier: The Machine and the Grand Design.

COUNCIL FOR BRITISH ARCHAEOLOGY (C.B.A.)

Formed in 1944 as the co-ordinating body for archaeological societies and opinion in the country. Included in its objects are the strengthening of measures to protect ancient monuments (q.v.) and historic buildings, including industrial remains. It also provides liaison between bodies concerned with these matters, promotes archaeological research. The Council administers grants for training in archaeological field techniques, provides information on facilities for those wishing to assist at excavations and has an archaeological abstracts service.

ADDRESS
Council for British Archaeology, 8, St Andrew's Place, London, N.W.1.

CORE

A word used to describe the heart of any large city or town. Smaller than what is generally understood as the Central Area, it contains the highest land values, the most intense building development per acre and the highest concentration of pedestrians and vehicles.

THE COUNCIL FOR THE PROTECTION OF RURAL ENGLAND

Was formed in 1926, though C.P.R.E. then stood for the Council for the Preservation of Rural England. It came into being to bring together the various national bodies interested in different parts of the English countryside.

C.P.R.E.'s objects are to protect the beauty of the English country from disfigurement and injury; to act as a centre for obtaining and giving advice and information on matters affecting the protection of rural scenery; to rouse public opinion to an understanding of the importance of this work and of the need to promote it.

The C.P.R.E. has forty-six constituent bodies and, with headquarters in London, it is represented locally by thirty-nine branches and County Committees. Both the constituent bodies and the branches appoint two representatives on the General Council. The Executive committee is elected annually and the majority of its members are selected from these representatives.

The C.P.R.E., like the Civic Trust (q.v.), is a charity and receives no direct government grant. There are equivalent bodies for Wales (C.P.R.W.) and Scotland (C.P.R.S.).

ADDRESSES

C.P.R.E., 4, Hobart Place, London, S.W.1.
C.P.R.W., Meifoel, Montgomery.
C.P.R.S., 39–43, Castle Street, Edinburgh, 2.

COUNTRY PARKS

Country Parks are being established under the 1968 Countryside Act, by the Countryside Commission (q.v.) as one way of promoting and facilitating public enjoyment of the countryside. These can be areas of land, acquired by Local Authorities (including County Boroughs outside whose boundaries the land might lie) or still in private ownership. The Commission can give grants of 75 per cent of expenditure so long as its slender resources permit.

Country parks can vary very considerably in size. Of the 70 established by the end of 1970, the variation was between 20 and 100 acres.

The principal aim of these parks is to provide the urban dweller with opportunities to enjoy the countryside by short walks, picnics, or just sitting and enjoying the view. Consequently they are normally within easy reach of main centres of population.

A secondary aim, though very important, is to relieve pressure on the National Parks (q.v.) and reduce the conflict of interests that arises when numbers of people (often town-dwellers) wish to use for recreational purposes land that is really the workshop for the rural population.

FURTHER READING
Countryside Commission (1969). *Policy on Country Parks and Picnic Sites.*

COUNTRYSIDE COMMISSION

Suggested in the White Paper 'Leisure in the Countryside' and subsequently established by the Countryside Act 1968 to replace the National Parks Commission. For England and Wales it is a department under the Dept of the Environment, funded directly from it but having a separate board of commissioners drawn from various sections of the community concerned in one way or another with the countryside. Scotland's Commission is responsible to its Secretary of State. The commissions are served by full-time staff, are charged with overseeing the provision and improvement of facilities for the enjoyment of the countryside and securing a proper conservation of its beauty. Public access to and enjoyment of the countryside for recreational purposes has to be secured too.

So National Parks (q.v.), Areas of Outstanding Natural Beauty (q.v.), Country Parks (q.v.) are all the responsibility of the Commissions. In addition they are expected to provide technical information for local authorities and a flow of information to secure among the general public a much better understanding of the countryside. Included in this information is the Countryside Code, a ten-point reminder about proper behaviour in the countryside.

ADDRESSES

Countryside Commission, 1, Cambridge Gate, Regents Park, London, N.W.1 4JY.
Countryside Commission for Scotland, Branklyn House, 116, Dundee Road, Perth.

FURTHER READING
Countryside Act 1968.
Countryside Commission Annual Reports.

opposite
Country Parks
10. & 11. Elvaston Castle Country Park: The first in the United Kingdom

COUNTY BOROUGH COUNCIL (*see* Local Government).

COUNTY COUNCIL (*see* Local Government).

COUNTY MAP

The basic document required from every county planning authority under the 1947 Town and Country Planning Act. Usually to a scale of 1″ to 1 mile it indicated in broad outline the land use and transportation networks for a county area. In practice it was found that the map did not inform the Minister or the public about the authority's long term intentions for the area (because of its Ordnance Survey base); neither did it inform property owners and developers how their interests were to be affected or where the opportunities for development lay. In effect the map's usefulness was confined to illustrating road systems, showing areas of special landscape importance and acting as a key for town maps.

With local Planning authorities now operating the 1968 Town and Country Planning Act, the County Map has now been superseded by Structure Plans (q.v.).

FURTHER READING

Cullingworth, J. B. (3rd Ed. 1969). *Town and Country Planning in England and Wales.*
Keeble, Lewis. (4th Ed. 1969). *Principles and Practice of Town and Country Planning.*
Ministry of Housing and Local Government. (1970). *Development Plans.*

COVENTRY

Notorious elsewhere for the behaviour of one of its earlier citizens this city has achieved an indelible place in British (and even international) planning thought. Presented with the progressively worsening problems of urban expansion and a city centre that could not cope with the demands placed upon it, the city fathers took the bold step of appointing a city architect, Donald Gibson (q.v.). In 1938 it was an exceptional step and the Architectural Department created attracted many keen and highly trained

people. Plans, ideas and models were prepared and discussed with many organisations and in the schools. Progress was slowed by the need to help with Civil Defence and housing for war workers and the plan was little further forward when the city centre was blasted out of existence by the air attack of 14 November 1940. Within three weeks, Lord Reith, Minister of Works and Buildings, had selected Coventry as one of three blitzed areas for study, to assist in defining what new planning legislation would be required for reconstruction.

The City Council was asked to prepare a comprehensive scheme for this purpose. Architect and Engineer were instructed to collaborate but, owing to fundamentally different attitudes, were unable to do so and presented two schemes to the committee. The Council adopted the Architect's scheme and submitted it to the Minister.

The plan embodied a number of basic ideas at a time when any sort of planning technique was in its infancy. Rejecting some of the ideas of Le Corbusier (q.v.) as being irrelevant to the centre of a small city, the planners adopted the idea of surrounding the central area with a parkway (q.v.). Within this there was to be no industrial development and uses would be grouped into several precincts (q.v.). Reacting to the impact of Lewis Mumford's thoughts in *The Culture of Cities* the planners sought to keep main uses where they had always been and created a new sort of traffic-free shopping centre which reflected something of the two level form at Chester (see Four Towns Reports). Around this were grouped theatres, markets, two level car parking. A great new square, a small central park and some high density (q.v.) housing.

Conceived as a set of principles, Coventry anticipated many of the suggestions later to appear in the publication of the Ministry of Town and Country Planning called *Handbook on the Redevelopment of Central Areas.* Today the interest in Coventry is that many of the original ideas have been realised.

FURTHER READING

Johnson-Marshall, Percy (1966). *Rebuilding Cities.*

C.P.R.E. (*see* Council for the Protection of Rural England).

CUMBERNAULD

Probably the most controversial British New Town to date. Planned by Sir Hugh Wilson, when Chief Architect and Planner to the Development Corporation, the main features of the town are its dramatic town centre, its totally segregated system of pedestrian and vehicular traffic, and its above average housing density. In each of these features it is markedly different from the earlier New Towns (q.v.).

The town centre is set on the brow of a hill, and planned on eight different levels, connected by lifts, ramps and escalators. At ground level there are covered bus stops and parking areas and on the upper level shops, offices, restaurants, cinemas, maisonettes and penthouse flats.

The safety of the town centre is matched throughout the town, the sophisticated system of highways, flyovers, grade separated inter-sections (q.v.) being complemented by an intricate system of footpaths and underpasses for pedestrians.

Grouped around the town centre, within easy walking distance, are houses and flats, all carefully grouped to give maximum privacy and views across the hills. A little further away there are three 'villages' with their own facilities. The original village of Cumbernauld has been retained with sensitivity and skill.

Cumbernauld has become world famous and claimed by many to be the quintessence of the New Town idea. But it is not without its critics who dislike its sober tones and the so-called 'contrived' Town Centre.

FURTHER READING
Osborn, F. J. and Whittick, Arnold (2nd Ed. 1969). *New Towns: The Answer to Megalopolis.*

12. Cumbernauld New Town: The town centre

D

DECAY

That process, as yet largely uncharted and whose causes are not fully identified, whereby property (buildings and land) declines in appearance, and structural stability, and the surrounding area suffers social degeneration: a process which is linked to but not entirely explained simply by the ageing of materials.

FURTHER READING
Medhurst, Franklin and Parry-Lewis, John (1969). *Urban Decay.*

DELEGATED POWERS

Those powers, given by Parliament to one Local Authority which may, at that Authority's discretion, be delegated to another, lower authority in the Local Government (q.v.) hierarchy.

In planning parlance the term usually refers to powers of Development Control (q.v.) delegated by the County Planning Authority to a District Council (q.v.) (either Urban or Rural).

FURTHER READING
Ministry of Housing and Local Government. Circular 58/59.

DECENTRALIZATION

The redistribution of population or land uses from a highly concentrated point to a wider area or into different pre-planned zones. An example of decentralisation is the distribution of office accommodation from London to other regional areas.

DENSITY

The number of people or the amount of accommodation per unit area of ground. The density of residential areas is usually expressed in terms of people or rooms per acre, and may be *gross* or *net* according to whether ancillary uses such as school sites and public open space are included. The density of business and commercial areas is usually expressed in terms of *plot ratio* (q.v.) or *floor space index* (q.v.).

Although density cannot be used in isolation from other criteria it has become one of the most common forms of measurement. Much debate has occurred about what is an acceptable density for different land uses and for patterns of activity within those uses. Clearly they vary from one part of the world to another, but in the U.K. most new residential development does not exceed 120 persons to the acre (gross) and can be as low as 20 p.p.a. By contrast, densities in Hong Kong often exceed 1,000 persons per acre. (*See also* High Rise)

FURTHER READING
James, J. R. (1967). *Residential Densities and Housing Layouts.*
Jenson, Rolf. (1966). *High Density Living.*

DERELICT LAND

The definition of derelict land given by the Secretary of State for the Environment can be summed up as follows:

'Land so damaged by industrial or other development that it is incapable of beneficial use without treatment.'

(For the present most ideas of derelict land relate to the aftermath of mineral workings (coal or chemical ore) or heavy manufacturing industry. No one has yet suggested that surplus land from now discontinued railway lines is derelict, but it may yet prove to be so.)

In 1971 it was estimated that some 99,000 acres were derelict, the majority of which were

opposite
13. Decay

in Lancs and the West Riding of Yorkshire, the Black Country and Tyneside. It has been estimated that Britain's wasteland increases by about 3,500 acres a year.

Although Government aid is available (85 per cent in Development districts (q.v.) and 75 per cent in Intermediate Areas (q.v.), Areas of Outstanding Natural Beauty (q.v.) and National Parks (q.v.)) it is unevenly so and many needy areas do not qualify. And local authorities have so many claims on their resources that much of the work is beyond them.

FURTHER READING
Barr, John (1969). *Derelict Britain.*
Civic Trust (1964). *Derelict Land.*
Oxenham, J. R. (1966). *Reclaiming Derelict Land.*
N.W. Economic Planning Council (1970). *Derelict Land.*

DESIGNATED AREAS
An area marked on a map and indicating land required by a Ministry, public body or a local authority and therefore liable to compulsory purchase within ten years (or seven years in the case of agricultural land).

This provision is made under the planning legislation of 1947–67 inclusive. The 1968 Town and Country Planning Act removes the right of designation.

The existence, or not, of designated areas, however, in no way prejudices any power of compulsory acquisition *otherwise* available to the acquiring authority.

FURTHER READING
Keeble, Lewis (4th Ed. 1969). *Principles and Practice of Town and Country Planning.*

DEVELOPMENT
Is a key word in the understanding of town and country planning in Britain. All 'development'

is subject to planning control and its legal definition is 'the carrying out of building, engineering, mining or other operations in, on or under the land, or the making of any material change of use of any building or other land'. This definition is very comprehensive and covers almost anything from a multi-storey building to the erection of an advertisement hoarding.

However, some kinds of development do not require planning permission and are definitely exempted. They include work connected with forestry and agriculture, road works and some, though not all, minor types of development. These are listed in the Use Classes Order (q.v.) and the General Development Order (q.v.). Where a local authority feels that development in one of these classes is likely to impair the environment or have a harmful planning effect it may bring it within the effect of the Town and Country Planning Acts by making an Article 4 Direction (q.v.) of the General Development Order.

FURTHER READING
Cullingworth, J. B. (3rd Ed. 1970). *Town and Country Planning in England and Wales.*
Heap, Desmond (5th Ed. 1969). *An Outline of Planning Law.*

DEVELOPMENT AREAS (*see* Assisted Areas).

DEVELOPMENT CONTROL
The process by which a planning authority exercises its statutory duty to control all development in accordance with the provisions of its development plan (q.v.). The control is possible by virtue of the obligation upon all developers to seek planning consent for new development. Applications may be granted, granted with conditions, or refused. Aggrieved applicants may appeal to the Secretary of State for the Environment.

In exercising its development control powers (often delegated by County Councils (q.v.) to District Councils under Part III of the 1962 Town and Country Planning Act) the local authority must have regard to its development

opposite
14. Derelict Land: Ashton in Makerfield, Lancs
15. Derelict Land Reclaimed: Bedfordshire Brickfields

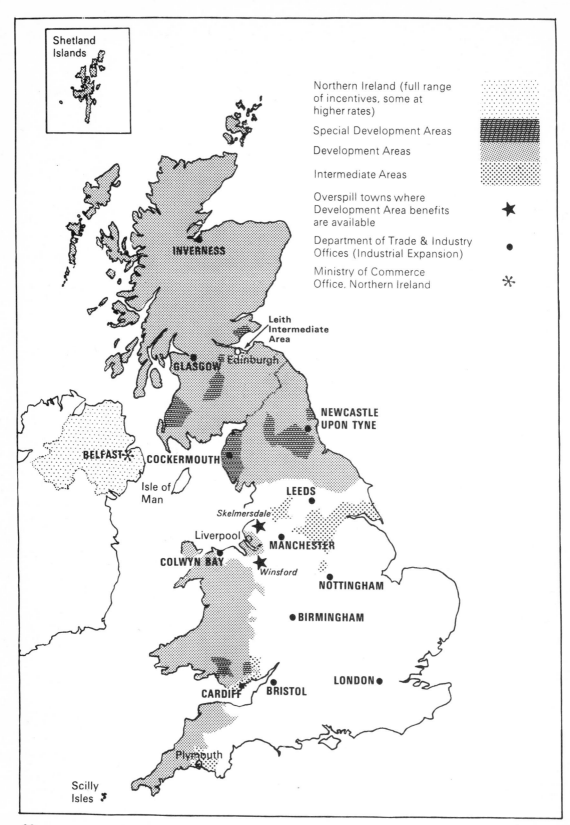

Shetland Islands

Northern Ireland (full range of incentives, some at higher rates)

Special Development Areas

Development Areas

Intermediate Areas

Overspill towns where Development Area benefits are available ★

Department of Trade & Industry Offices (Industrial Expansion) ●

Ministry of Commerce Office, Northern Ireland ✳

INVERNESS

Leith Intermediate Area

GLASGOW   Edinburgh

NEWCASTLE UPON TYNE

BELFAST   COCKERMOUTH

Isle of Man

LEEDS

Skelmersdale

Liverpool   MANCHESTER

COLWYN BAY   Winsford

NOTTINGHAM

BIRMINGHAM

LONDON

CARDIFF   BRISTOL

Plymouth

Scilly Isles

plan but is not confined solely to it and may have regard to other material considerations.

Development Control, often badly or unimaginatively administered, is, probably more than any other, the main reason for planning as a whole experiencing a certain unpopularity. It has often been far too negative and whilst in many instances it has prevented monstrous proposals being implemented it has also been responsible for stifling scores of imaginative ideas. The 17,000+ appeals per annum (1967 figures) indicate a fairly extensive dissatisfaction with Development Control as at present administered.

(See Planning Applications. Planning Appeals, Delegated Powers.)

FURTHER READING

Central Office of Information (1968). *Town and Country Planning in Britain*

Cullingworth, J. B. (3rd Ed. 1970). *Town and Country Planning in England and Wales.*

Heap, Desmond (5th Ed. 1969). *An Outline of Planning Law.*

Keeble, Lewis (4th Ed. 1969). *Principles and Practice of Town and Country Planning.*

Little, A. J. (1969). *The Enforcement of Planning Control.*

DEVELOPMENT PLAN

The name given to the set of documents (maps, sketches and a written statement) prepared by each Local Planning Authority (q.v.) as a Legal requirement of the Town and Country Planning Act 1962. The development plan shows how it is intended (by the Local Planning Authority) that land shall be used including areas for housing, industry and recreation and sites for hospitals and schools. It is intended to inform developers and guide the local authority in its Development Control (q.v.).

Development Plans have to indicate some notion of programming. Under the 1947 Town and Country Planning Act, when they were first introduced, they were to be reviewed

every five years. Based Ordnance Survey Maps (6″ to the mile for the Town Maps (q.v.), 1″ to the mile for County Maps (q.v.), and 1 : 2500 for C.D.A.'s (q.v.)), they soon came in for criticism in that they were at one and the same time too inaccurate in not being able to show actual street widths etc., and too precise in enabling individual properties to be identified; and they failed to relate land use and traffic needs. Furthermore the administrative process whereby every plan and any substantial alteration to it had to be approved by the Minister (now Secretary of State for the Environment) was cumbersome and protracted.

The Town and Country Planning Act 1968 sought to remedy this in suggesting new sorts of plans [Structure and Local Planning (q.v.)] and by delegating to local planning authorities the right to determine their own local plans—though Structure Plans still have to receive ministerial approval.

FURTHER READING

Heap, Desmond (5th Ed. 1969). *An Outline of Planning Law.*

Ministry of Housing and Local Government (1970). *Development Plans.*

DISCONTINUANCE ORDER

A Discontinuance Order to prevent a particular activity may be made by a local planning authority (q.v.) 'if it appears . . . that it is expedient in the interests of the proper planning of their area (including the interests of amenity)'. Ministerial confirmation is necessary and full compensation (q.v.) has to be paid. Orders can be applied to any development, whether previously expressly permitted or dating from prior to the Planning Acts, but the Minister has shown by past decisions that only strong cases will be supported and the compensation costs have prevented many orders being made, except in the case of advertisements where compensation is slight.

opposite
16. Development Areas. Additional intermediate areas designated, March 1972

DISTRICT COUNCIL (*see* Local Government).

DOXIADIS, Constantinos 1913–
Greek Architect,
Educated at Athens Technical University, School of Architecture and Berlin—Charlottenburg University.

Principally known for his evolution of the theory of Ekistics (q.v.). His activities are impressive. Chief Town Planning Officer Athens, 1937–8. Head of Department of Regional and Town Planning, Ministry of Public Works 1939–45, and Acting Professor of Town Planning, Athens Technical University 1939–1943. Minister of Housing and Under-Secretary of Reconstruction 1945–8. Co-ordinator, Greek Recovery Programme 1948–51. Chairman, Board of Directors, Athens Technological Organisation 1958– . President, Doxiadis Associates Int. Co. Ltd., Consultant on Development and Ekistics, Athens 1951. Member Delegate, International Conference on Housing, Planning and Reconstruction 1947. Head of Delegation to Greco-Italian War Reparations Conference 1949–50. Delegate, Housing, Building and Planning Committee of Economic and Social Council of U.N. 1963–1964. Chairman, Session on Urban Problems, U.N. Conference on Application of Science and Technology for the benefit of Less Developed Areas, 1963. Consultant to U.N., I.A.D.B., A.I.D., I.B.R.D., I.C.A., Ford Foundation, Redevelopment Land Agency (Washington) and Governments of Brazil, Cyprus, Ethiopia, France, Ghana, Greece, India, Iran, Iraq, Jordan, Lebanon, Libya, Pakistan, Saudi Arabia, Spain, Sudan, Syria, U.S.A., S. Vietnam, Zambia. Numerous honorary degrees:

Sir Patrick Abercrombie Prize, International Union of Architects, Cali de Oro Award, Society of Mexican Architects, Industrial Designers Society of America Award of Excellence, Aspen Award 1966.

Not just a theorist, Doxiadis has been responsible for a number of major projects. They include: National ekistic, and housing programmes for Iraq, Lebanon and Libya. Plans and development programmes for Islamabad, Pakistan, Greater Rio de Janeiro, Accra-Tema Region, Ghana, Greater Khartoum, Baghdad; urban renewal and development plans for several U.S. cities; new campus of University of Punjab; Agricultural University of Lyallpur, Pakistan; new buildings for Agricultural University of Athens; survey for International Asian highway; design of highways in Greece; design and supervision of construction of airports in Libya, housing projects in Iraq, Pakistan, Libya, Greece, etc.

Doxiadis' publications include

> *Ekistic Analysis* (1946).
> *Destruction of Towns and Villages in Greece* (1947).
> *A Plan for the Survival of the Greek Peoples* (1957).
> *Our Capital and its Future* (1960).
> *Architecture in Transition* (1963).
> *The New World of Urban Man* (1965).
> *Urban Renewal and the Future of the American City* (1966).
> *Ekistics—An Introduction to the Science of Human Settlements* (1968).

E

EASEMENT

Easement, in law, is the name given to a person's right to restrict the freedom of another's use of land, or to guarantee his own use of it. So an easement may give the right to engage in limited activity on the land of another such as the privilege of maintaining and using a road or pipeline (affirmative easement); it might be a legal power given to one to prevent the owner of a piece of land from erecting a structure so as to obstruct light or air (negative easement).

The kinds of easement that may exist are as numerous as the uses to which land may be put. Rights that were clearly related to a pastoral or agrarian society have naturally become less common, only to be replaced by such rights as that of the free flight of aircraft at a prescribed height over land.

FURTHER READING
Anstey, Brian and Chavasse, Michael. *The Right to Light.*

EDINBURGH

Edinburgh, capital of Scotland, owes its place in any account of the history of planning to its New Town which, with the possible exception of Bath (q.v.) is the finest example of eighteenth- and nineteenth-century town improvement or extension anywhere in Britain.

The New Town is also the outcome of a combination of private enterprise and local government initiative. It was the city council which, in 1763, drained the North Loch (where the railway now runs south of Princes Street) and built North Bridge to connect the medieval hill city with the undeveloped land to its north, and it was they who, with the same determination to improve the appearance of their city, opened the planning of development on this land to competition.

The winning plan (1767) by James Craig has a clarity and scale in strong contrast to the medieval city. George Street, the widest street, forms its spine and runs along a crest at the highest point of the site. It is terminated by two squares, St Andrew's Square and Charlotte Square, and paralleled to north and south by Queen Street and Princes Street. Other streets run perpendicular to these to form development blocks which are served by mews. The outer sides of Queen and Princes Streets were to be kept free of development so as to retain views of the North Loch and the Firth of Forth. No such rigidly rectilinear framework had been planned on such a scale in Britain before.

Its rigidity has been slightly reduced, however, by the character of the architecture that clothes it. Uncertain of the demand for properties the council made little attempt to develop the New Town with architecturally unified pieces like those at Bath (where demand was assured). The only large scale entity is Charlotte Square designed by Robert Adam in 1790 when the success of the development was guaranteed.

Elsewhere development was piecemeal. But in order to ensure an overall unity of appearance the council drew up a number of regulations. Buildings along the principal streets could not exceed three storeys, those along lesser streets, two storeys; all had to conform to a uniform building line. Overhanging projections and dormer windows were prohibited, pavements had to be ten feet wide, building had to proceed within one year of site acquisition, and a sewer had to be provided along the centre of George Street. All the architects were also working within the same prevailing mode, employing common elements and using the same locally quarried sandstone. With the exception of Princes Street and the south and west of St Andrew's Square most of the buildings still stand today. They create a unified yet unregimented environment in which individual expression has been constrained and shaped, but not stifled, by an overall design policy. It is an achievement from which it is still possible to learn.

The later nineteenth century extensions of the New Town to north, east and west are freer and less rectilinear in plan, with their crescents, circuses and greater emphasis on landscape elements showing the influence of the Wood schemes for Bath. It is, however, a testament to the powerful and consistent character of Craig's original New Town that they form a distinct and identifiable architectural unity with it.

FURTHER READING
Mumford, Lewis (1961). *The City in History.*
Youngson, A. J. (1966). *The Making of Classical Edinburgh.*

EKISTICS

The science of human settlements. A term conceived by C. A. Doxiadis (q.v.) which embodies a pattern for the development of communities of all sizes. The term is derived from the Greek words Oikos meaning 'home' and Oiku meaning 'settling down'. The term was first used in a series of lectures given at the Athens Technical University in 1942.

Doxiadis went on to develop the Ekistic Logarithmic Scale (E.L.S.) which is a classification of settlements according to their size on the basis of a logarithmic scale, running from Man (Unit 1), to the whole earth (Unit 15).

The scale was first presented in 1961 and coincided with Doxiadis' use of another expression 'Ecumenopolis'—the coming city that will, together with the corresponding open land, indispensable to man, cover the entire Earth as a continuous system forming a universal settlement.

It is the thesis of Ekistics that although man spends more time and money on his physical environment than anything else, seldom has a co-ordinated national result been obtained. Ekistics tries to fill the gap by widening the planning to everything from dwelling units to regions to bring together not only the architect, the engineer, the planner, but also the sociologist, the economist, geographer and other specialists.

FURTHER READING
Doxiadis, C. A. (1968). 'Ekistics'—An introduction to the Science of Human Settlements.

ENFORCEMENT NOTICE

If a local planning authority believes that development (q.v.) has occurred without consent or in a manner which ignores conditions attached to the consent granted, it may serve an enforcement notice. This requires the developer to restore the property to its former state or comply with the conditions. If he wishes, the developer may follow another course of action; he can apply for planning permission and has a subsequent right of appeal if permission is refused. As proceedings following the service of an enforcement notice are often prolonged a local planning authority can prevent further work being carried out by serving a 'stop notice' in conjunction with the Enforcement Notice.

FURTHER READING
Little, A. J. (1969). The Enforcement of Planning Control.

ENVIRONMENT

A much over-used word to describe, in planning terms, the general comfort, convenience and aesthetic quality of the physical surroundings for living.

FURTHER READING
Arvil, Robert (Rev. Ed. 1969). Man and Environment.
Hopkins, Muriel F. S. (1968). Learning through the Environment. Education Today Series.
Nicholson, Max (1969). Environmental Revolution.
Rowland, Kurt (1964–5). Development of Shape. Pattern and Shape. Shape of Towns. Shapes we need. Looking and Seeing Series.

ENVIRONMENTAL AREA

Originally, as used in the Buchanan (q.v.) Report Traffic in Towns, an area having no extraneous traffic, and within which considerations of environment predominate over the use of vehicles. Now generalised to mean an area of sufficient aesthetic quality or unity to merit it being considered as a whole.

FURTHER READING
Ministry of Transport (1963). Traffic in Towns. (Buchanan Report).

ENVIRONMENTAL RECOVERY

A fairly recent term used to describe the idea of rehabilitating whole districts. Most obviously applicable in the older industrial areas of the U.K., the technique involves selecting an area of housing and other mixed uses, still structurally sound but lacking certain amenities. Following this an assessment is made of which properties may be retained and which must be demolished. Some demolition is usually

opposite
Environmental Recovery
17 & 18. Skelmersdale, Lancs, before and after

inevitable in order to secure space for play areas, landscaping, etc.

The properties are then rehabilitated, often with some new building to provide bathroom/kitchen/bedroom extensions. The environment is improved by closing some streets to traffic, re-paving, planting, providing parking and/or garage facilities.

The improvement of houses is actively encouraged by central government in the form of grants (q.v.) and private owners/occupiers and landlords can implement the improvements to the houses. Improvement of the environment generally has to be planned for and implemented by the Local Authority and can be aided if the authority declares a General Improvement Area (q.v.). The 1969 Housing Act is directed almost entirely at enabling this sort of rehabilitation to take place.

During 1968 a number of pilot schemes were started. In Rochdale the Ministry of Housing and Local Government managed a scheme which carried out certain environmental improvements and resulted in a number of individuals improving their houses. Another pilot scheme, managed by the Civic Trust for the North West, sought to actively sponsor and co-ordinate improvements to property and the environment by private owners and the local authority in the old part of Skelmersdale. Others were undertaken at Whitworth, Lancashire and Exeter, Devon.

The technical problems of Environmental Recovery are much less taxing than the managerial difficulties. The cost benefit studies which show favourably for Environmental Recovery have resulted in efforts being re-doubled to overcome these managerial difficulties, though progress is slow.

FURTHER READING
Civic Trust for the North West (1969). *Environmental Recovery at Skelmersdale.*
Ministry of Housing and Local Government (1966). *The Deeplish Study.*
Hallmark Securities Ltd (1966). *The Halliwell Report.*

EQUIVALENT RE-INSTATEMENT
The principle which requires that a Local Planning Authority, when it disturbs an existing use should, as compensation (q.v.), provide equivalent accommodation, or the means to it.

This applies to land uses or buildings that would not normally be negotiable in the open market, such as Churches, Chapels, hostels, etc.

FURTHER READING
Heap, Desmond (5th Ed. 1969). *An Outline of Planning Law.*

F

FLOOR SPACE INDEX
F.S.I. is an alternative to Plot Ratio (q.v.) as a way of expressing density in non-residential areas. The Index is established by dividing the area of the total floor-space of the buildings on any particular site by the site area, including half the area of any roads adjoining it.

The use of F.S.I. has declined in recent years.

FOOTPATHS
Legally protected rights of way, in town or country, providing the pedestrian with a quick, safe and usually pleasant route between two points. Footpaths are part of the Queen's highway.

Though they are often neglected and sometimes illegally blocked or closed by landowners, footpaths that are shown on the definitive statutory maps that County Councils (q.v.) are supposed to prepare, are maintainable by the Highway Authorities. The statutory maps also show whether the path is a genuine footpath (i.e. for pedestrians only) or a bridleway (on which horses and cyclists are also allowed).

If a footpath runs through a site that is to be developed, the proposal to stop up the path has to be advertised. In the absence of any objections the Local Planning Authority (q.v.) may authorise closure. If there are objections, the proposed closing (or diversion) has to be referred to the Secretary of State for the Environment.

FURTHER READING

Garner, J. F. (2nd Ed. 1969). *Rights of Way and Access to the Countryside.*

Ministry of Housing and Local Government (1968). *Report of the Footpaths Committee* (Gosling Report).

Wright, C. J. (1967). *A Guide to the Pennine Way.*

FORESTRY COMMISSION

Founded in 1919. The Forestry Commissioners are charged with the general duty of promoting the interests of forestry, the development of afforestation, the production and supply of timber and the maintenance of reserves of growing trees in Great Britain. Including the former Crown woods transferred to it in 1924, the Commission has acquired about 2,700,000 acres of land (70 per cent being plantable) of which 1,600,000 acres are under plantation. Under various grant schemes, financial assistance is given to private owners and local authorities in respect of approved works of afforestation.

There have been times when the interests of the Commission have brought it into conflict with preservationists and country lovers who have resented the often harsh planting pattern adopted by the Commission. In recent years, however, there has been a notable change and, with landscape consultants advising, the com-

19. A Forestry Commission plantation

mission has been able to continue to discharge its responsibilities and often make a real contribution to improved landscape.

ADDRESS
Forestry Commission, 25, Savile Row, London W1X 2AY.

FURTHER READING
Crowe, Sylvia (2nd Imp. 1963). *Tomorrow's Landscape.*
Fairbrother, Nan (1970). *New Lives New Landscapes.*
Miles, Roger (1967). *Forestry in the English Landscape.*

FORT WORTH (*see* Gruen, Victor).

FOUR TOWN REPORTS
In 1966 the Minister of Housing and Local Government set up a Preservation Policy Group (q.v.) and commissioned four pilot studies of the conservation problems in the historical centres of Bath (q.v.), Chester, Chichester and York. The reports, published in 1968, have become known as the Four Towns Reports.

In each of them the causes of physical decay in the historical environment and the threats to its conservation were found to be very similar. All the cities suffer from traffic congestion and its attendant noise and pollution; from a general exodus of the population to the suburbs and consequent under-use of basements and upper storeys; from inadequate investment in preservation of old and valuable buildings; and from poor design standards in new development. All the reports also agree in identifying traffic as the most fundamental problem, in that its reduction by conventional methods, which often include demolishing buildings, must almost invariably be resisted.

The solutions and proposals differ, however. The York Report (by Lord Esher) recommends strict controls on traffic entering the city, car parks strategically sited near the medieval walls and the removal of non-conforming industry, as essential pre-requisites for a policy

of attracting people, and especially students, back to the city centre, and suggests that some of these measures and other physical improvements to the environment could be financed by extra charges on hotel bills and museum admission fees and by exchequer subsidy.

The Chester Report (Donald Insall) recommends that the local authority should carry out some redevelopment schemes in decaying areas, sometimes in partnership with private owners or housing societies, and with buildings being purchased, where necessary, by a proposed national historic towns corporation similar to the then existing Land Commission.

By contrast, the Bath Report (Colin Buchanan (q.v.) and Partners), is convinced that conservation costs will eventually be recouped by an expanded tourist trade and that the local authority, and not any national body, is therefore the proper instrument for conservation policies. It recommends that exchequer finance should be made available to help the local authority purchase buildings for renovation and conversion and to subsidise long term traffic improvements.

The Chichester Report (G. S. Burrows) suggests restricting vehicular access to the city centre to two areas and introducing an electric minibus service elsewhere. It recommends that Trust Associations (rather than the local authority or any national body) should be empowered to purchase properties at existing use value for restoration and improvement, and that means of reducing rates in Conservation Areas (q.v.) should be explored.

These various measures were considered by the Preservation Policy Group and influenced the recommendations it put forward to the Minister in 1970 for changes in various aspects of national conservation policy. Pilot schemes have proceeded in each of the four cities.

Although the common problems identified in each of the reports indicate that all historic towns have certain shared problems, it has been suggested that the four towns selected were too similar in character, and in the pressures for change with which they are faced, and that an opportunity was missed for commissioning a study of a smaller historic town less subject to these pressures or of a small historic area surviving in one of our large Victorian industrial cities. A fifth report on King's Lynn was in fact originally intended but was abandoned as the local authority had just accepted the report of an independent consultant.

GARNIER, Tony 1869–1948

French architect and theorist whose project for an imaginary *Cité Industrielle*, designed between 1898 and 1904, was one of the earliest and most comprehensively thought out attempts to illustrate that complete acceptance of the requirements of a fully industrialised and technological society need not be incompatible with the creation of hygienic cities of ordered elegance and urbanity.

The project incorporated many ideas that have since become fundamental to modern planning theory. There is distinct functional zoning throughout, with the residential and public buildings situated on a central plateau and the industrial buildings, a hospital, a railway station and an existing old town separated from it and each other by green belts. To the north a dam and hydroelectric plant provide power for the whole city.

In the residential districts simple cubic houses without enclosed private greens or backyards are placed within continuous and traffic-free green areas. Each has at least one bedroom window facing south and occupies no more than half its plot. Each residential district has its primary school. The linear shape of the whole city is determined by the 'grid of parallel and perpendicular streets'. Pedestrian routes run independently of them. Public buildings, zoned separately from the houses, are further classified into three main groups: administrative and assembly buildings, entertainment centres and museums.

Architectural treatment is no less revolutionary. Although reinforced concrete construction was rare in 1900, Garnier envisaged its use in all important buildings throughout his city and visualised the shapes that were to become a standard part of the vocabulary of modern architecture: flat and cantilevered roofs, continuous strips of glazing, *pilotis* and glass walls. Decoration is minimal.

In some respects the *Cité* is not dissimilar to the Garden Cities proposed by Ebenezer Howard (q.v.) in 1898 but the differences are more pronounced. Howard prescribes a maximum population of 32,000 while Garnier assumes a population of 35,000. But the *Cité* is designed for linear expansion. It is an idealisation of the big city idea. Garnier is as excited by the problem of designing for industry, commerce and transport as he is by those of improving housing conditions. His *Cité* is closer in spirit to the *Città Nuova* project of Sant'Elia (q.v.) than Howard's proposal and more consistently visualised than either.

Although mention of Garnier is now *de rigueur* in most books dealing with the development of modern architecture and planning, his influence is still largely uncharted. The exhibition of his project in Paris in 1904 and its later publication in expanded and modified form in 1917, ensured that his ideas became known in progressive architectural circles and his influence has also been discerned in the suburbs of Amsterdam, in Kvarnholmen in Sweden, in Russian garden cities and, where the connection is the least tenuous, in Leon Jaussely's project for Barcelona (1903). However, the only substantial link is with Le Corbusier (q.v.) who knew Garnier personally, discussed his work publicly and acknowledged his influence in his own plan for a City for Three Million People.

FURTHER READING
Pawlowski, Christophe (1967). *Tony Garnier*.
Wiebenson, Dora. *Tony Garnier: The Cité Industrielle*.

Pevsner, Nikolaus (1968). *The Sources of Modern Architecture and Design.*

Evenson, Norma (1969). *Le Corbusier: the machine and the Grand Design.*

GEDDES PATRICK Sir 1854–1932

Sir Patrick Geddes was both by training and inclination a biologist and sociologist. His biological work concentrated on the importance of sex in evolution, but in planning circles his indelible mark is made by his extensive contribution to fresh thought on the shape and location of contemporary human communities. He conducted extensive surveys in Scotland, India and Palestine and from them drew the conclusion that the development of human communities calls for plans that are based upon a thorough understanding of the impact on one another of people and their environment. The author of *Cities in Evolution* (1915), he may fairly be said to have influenced, almost more than any other thinker, the development of planning philosophy and certainly convinced whole generations of planners of the value of survey and plan! Mumford (q.v.) was a follower of Geddes and was deeply influenced by him.

A Scotsman, Geddes was born at Ballater, was knighted in 1931 and died in France in 1932.

GENERAL DEVELOPMENT ORDER (G.D.O.)

In the 1947 Town and Country Planning Act (and in the subsequent Acts) the Minister was empowered to make an order listing certain types of activities that did not require planning permission. If a proposed development falls within these classes then no application for planning permission is needed as the General Development Order itself is the permission. There is a distinction between this order and the Use Classes Order (q.v.): the G.D.O. lists development (q.v.) which is permitted whilst the Use Classes Order lists those changes of use which do not constitute development.

FURTHER READING
Heap, Desmond (5th Ed. 1969). *An Outline of Planning Law.*

GEORGIAN GROUP

The Georgian Group exists to stimulate public appreciation of Georgian architecture and town planning and to save from destruction or disfigurement Georgian squares, terraces, streets and individual buildings of special architectural merit. It is also available to advise owners and public authorities on the preservation and repair of Georgian buildings and on the uses to which they can, if necessary, be adapted. The Group does not advocate the erection of modern buildings in a Georgian or neo-Georgian style but, where an area is replanned, it seeks to ensure that new buildings harmonise with the old.

The Group was founded by Lord Derwent in 1937 and is a registered charity dependent financially on subscribing members. The term 'Georgian' is used for convenience to cover all architecture designed in the classical idiom.

ADDRESS
The Georgian Group. 2, Chester Street, London SW1.

GENERAL IMPROVEMENT AREA (G.I.A.)

See Improvement Area.

GIBBERD, Sir Frederick, 1908–

Architect, planner and author, Gibberd studied at Birmingham School of Architecture and entered private practice in 1930. He has designed a diverse range of individual buildings including Scunthorpe steel works (1947), London Airport (1955 to the present), Nuclear Power Stations at Hinkley Point (1961), and Sizewell, Suffolk, several housing schemes, technical colleges and flats, St Albans Civic Centre, and Liverpool Metropolitan Cathedral (1960) which shows the influence of Oscar Niemeyer's Cathedral at Brasilia (q.v.). His place in the present book is due, however, more to his work as planning consultant to several local authorities and his appointment, in 1947, as architect designer of Harlow New Town (q.v.). Gibberd's Master Plan for Harlow was the first of the new town plans to be approved

20. Sir Frederick Gibberd

sensitive regard for their natural settings, have contributed to the growing public acceptance of industrial complexes as potentially beautiful and exciting objects in the landscape.

Gibberd has written *The Architecture of England* (1938), a popular history of architecture, *Town Design* (1953), one of the first major works to discuss the art of town design and reflecting the work of Camillo Sitte (q.v.), and was co-author with Francis Yorke of *Modern Flats* (1958). He is a Member of the Royal Fine Art Commission (q.v.) and, between 1943 and 1945 was principal of the Architectural Association School of Architecture.

FURTHER READING
Creese, Walter L. (1966). *The Search for Environment. (The Garden City Before and After.)*

GIBSON, Sir Donald Evelyn Edward 1908–
Architect and planner who made a substantial contribution to the evolution of British planning theory and practice while City Architect of Coventry (1939–55) and County Architect of Nottinghamshire (1955–8).

Under Gibson's auspices at Nottinghamshire, a system for the prefabrication of schools was evolved to combat the effects of subsidence in mining areas and to allow schools to be built with mass-produced construction units at low cost. It was later exploited by the Consortium of Local Authorities Special Programme (C.L.A.S.P.). While this contributed to the speed with which the County's school building programme could be implemented and enabled individual schools to be planned with a flexibility suited to contemporary educational theory, Gibson's place in the annals of planning is due more to his work at Coventry (q.v.) where, following the German air raids during the Second World War, he was responsible for recreating the city centre. The new centre incorporates a multi-level and precinctual shopping complex and is generally recognised to have realised more of the opportunities presented by the blitz than any other major post-war reconstruction scheme in Britain.

On leaving Nottinghamshire, Gibson was

by the Minister of Local Government and Planning and his housing estate at Somerford Road, Hackney (1949) was the first planned mixed development to be built in England.

Other major developments Gibberd has designed include Lansbury Market, Poplar, and the re-creation of Nuneaton Town Centre following war damage in 1941.

Gibberd's ten storey block of flats, The Lawn, in the Mark Hall Neighbourhood of Harlow (1951), was one of the first 'high rise' (q.v.) point blocks in Britain for public housing and has been interpreted as an affirmation of post-war confidence. It shows the influence of Sweden and reflected a wish in the architectural profession to keep abreast with international developments. By providing a focal point in a predominantly low-lying neighbourhood, it also went some way to meet the criticisms of those who found the residential areas of the Mark I New Towns (q.v.) conspicuously lacking in visual compactness and identity.

It seems likely that the Power Stations at Hinkley Point and Sizewell, with their appointed Director General of Works in the War Office where he extended the C.L.A.S.P. prefabrication system for use in other buildings. He completed his career at the Ministry of Public Building and Works, first as Director General of Research and Development (1963–7) and finally, until his retirement in 1969, as Controller General. He was awarded the C.B.E. in 1951, became President of the Royal Institute of British Architects (q.v.) in 1959, and was knighted in 1962.

Gibson's formative years were spent at the school of architecture at Manchester University (1927–32) and at the Department of Civic Design under Sir Patrick Abercrombie (q.v.) at Liverpool University (1934).

FURTHER READING
Johnson-Marshall, Percy (1966). *Rebuilding Cities.*

21. Grade Separation: Snowhill Lane Bridge on M6

GRADE SEPARATION
A term to describe the carrying of one highway over or under another with or without facilities for interchange. Fly-over and underpass have the same meaning.

FURTHER READING
Drake, James (1969). *Motorways.*

GRANTS
Grants are financial donations from central or local government to assist worthwhile proposals. They are administered in different ways by different departments. Some are to enable local authorities to build schools, houses and hospitals. Others may be given to help with buildings that are unusually expensive in order to satisfy high aesthetic requirements, such as certain agricultural buildings that have to fit into the landscape. Other grants that are particularly related to the planning field are:
   (i) Grants for the repair or maintenance of

buildings of architectural or historical importance. If they are of outstanding importance they may attract a grant from the Historic Buildings Council (q.v.) which gives about £700,000 annually for this purpose. If the building is not 'outstanding' it may receive a grant from the Local Authority under the Local Authorities (Historic Buildings) Act 1962, though many councils provide no grants at all or, at best, very few.

(ii) Derelict Land (q.v.) Grants are available to local authorities to help them remedy the scars of abandoned industrial processes. The amount of the grant varies from 85 per cent in Development Areas (q.v.) 75 per cent in Intermediate Areas to 50 per cent elsewhere. Land Acquisition and Fees may be included in the figures used for grant assessment purposes.

(iii) Grants for the improvement of ordinary (i.e. not historically important) buildings, particularly housing are classified either as Standard or Discretionary Grants. *Standard Grants* are given to enable a houseowner to provide a house with five basic (or 'standard') amenities. The maximum is £200 and they are mandatory on the local authority. *Discretionary Grants* are given at the local council's discretion and are limited to half the cost of the approved works. The maximum grant is £1,500 per house (all transferable to the owner) plus a grant of up to £50 for environmental reasons provided the Local Authority matches it pound for pound. These grants cover almost every real improvement to a house.

FURTHER READING
Barr, John (1969). *Derelict Britain*.
Ministry of Housing and Local Government (1968). *Money to Modernise Your Home*.
Ministry of Housing and Local Government (1969). *Protecting our Historic Buildings*.

GREEN BELTS
Those areas around villages, towns or cities in which development is strictly controlled and usually not permitted at all. The Green Belt policy has proved a most useful device in preventing the endless sprawl of towns or the coagulation of one town with another, providing townspeople with a welcome release from the strain of city life, protecting the special character of some towns.

The policy has deficiencies. For example it encourages the leap-frogging of development over the Green Belt to the land (often White Land) (q.v.) beyond it. But it has become understood and accepted by the general public and no real alternative has yet been devised.

FURTHER READING
Best, Robin and Coppock, J. T. (2nd Imp. 1965). *The Changing Use of Land in Britain*.
Mandelker, Daniel R. (1962). *Green Belts and Urban Growth*.
Thomas, David (1970). *London's Green Belt*.

GREENWAYS
A rather vague description of landscaped high-speed (or motorway) (q.v.) roads. The idea is that the road should be flanked by continuous areas of green. Synonymous with 'Parkways'. (*See also* Parker, Barry).

GREENWICH VILLAGE
Originally a small village, subsequently a salubrious upper-class suburb frequented by artists and writers (among them Walt Whitman, Henry James and Mark Twain), Greenwich Village is now a fashionable bohemian district in Manhattan, New York, with narrow and winding streets, old buildings (some decaying, some renovated), exotic night clubs, restaurants, coffee bars, antique shops, used furniture stores and a population of mixed race, culture, class and income.

Probably the only internationally famous Twilight Zone (q.v.), it is taken by some writers on planning, notably Jane Jacobs (q.v.), as a standard by which to judge the success and vitality of more planned, less haphazard environments.

FURTHER READING
Jacobs, Jane (1962). *The Death and Life of Great American Cities*.
Glazer, Nathan (1958). 'Why City Planning is Obsolete'. Article in *Architectural Forum*. July '58.

GROPIUS, Walter, 1883–1969

Architect, industrial designer and cardinal figure in the development of modern architecture, Gropius owes his place in any account of the history of planning to his invention of the residential layout in which slab blocks of flats are placed laterally or obliquely to a street rather than parallel with it.

Described and advocated by Gropius in a number of articles and in his book *The New Architecture and the Bauhaus* (1935), the layout was a considered and original response to the related urban problems of sprawl and congestion. Gropius believed that the ideal of the detached house in its own garden would, if widely adopted, lead only to the eventual disintegration of the city. At the same time he recognised that the housing conditions prevailing in most cities, where terraces and tenement blocks were placed close together without greenery or adequate sunlight, were such as to make the ideal increasingly popular. His layout was therefore evolved in an attempt to retain urban character and high density while introducing amenities and a feeling of spaciousness that had hitherto been primarily confined to the suburb or the countryside. With comparative diagrams he demonstrated that two twelve-storey apartment blocks placed across a site with open space between them could achieve the same density per acre as twelve rows of conventional two-storey terrace houses and, further, that the higher the blocks became the less the angle of light between the base of one block and the roofline of the next and the greater the sunlight. The blocks themselves could be turned on the site to obtain maximum sunlight and the open space between them planted with trees or made into gardens as well as providing room for car parking.

Gropius was able to put his ideas into practice in part of the Dammerstock estate near Karlsruhe (q.v.), (1927–8) and, a year later and on a larger scale, at the Siemensstadt estate near Berlin. In both schemes he designed a number of apartment blocks while supervising the work of several other architects. Both were widely publicised and have been imitated in residential layouts throughout the world.

It is also likely that both *The New Architec-ture and the Bauhaus* and Gropius's contribution to the Third C.I.A.M. (q.v.) Conference in 1930 (where he argued the case for multi-storey apartment blocks) had a less attributable and more diffusive influence. It was a time when the word skyscraper tended to evoke an image of the cavernous streets and crammed skyline of Chicago and when there was considerable controversy about whether or not skyscrapers should be introduced into Europe. C.I.A.M. (q.v.) itself had called for a study of the economic and sociological implications of skyscraper construction. By demonstrating that the layout of tall buildings could be as carefully and thoughtfully planned as that of any other form of development, Gropius contributed towards an increasing acceptance of high rise (q.v.) development.

FURTHER READING

Gropius, W. (1935). *The New Architecture and the Bauhaus.*

Giedon, S. (1954). *Walter Gropius: Work and Teamwork.*

Fitch, J. M. (1960). *Walter Gropius.*

GRUEN, Victor, 1903–

Planner and author who has pioneered the development in America of both regional and city centre pedestrian shopping areas.

The regional shopping centre has developed in the U.S.A. in response to problems of town and city centre traffic congestion. Large areas of land, strategically sited near main roads and within easy reach of a large and mobile sub-urban population, are devoted exclusively to the provision of shopping facilities which are not aligned along roads but placed facing a pedestrian area in a central position within the site, and served by peripheral car parks connected to the road network. A few such centres had been built before the '50s, but Gruen was the first to give sustained thought to their function and detailed design and to consider them in planning rather than merely commercial terms. His Northland Centre near Detroit (1952) was the first in which the shops were clustered at the centre and encircled by car parks rather than placed on each side of a central strip, and

23. Victor Gruen: Sketch for Fort Worth Development

the fountains, flowerbeds, trees, street furniture (q.v.), and outdoor cafes with which it was furnished set a standard for all subsequent centres. At Southdale Centre near Minneapolis (1960), seeking inspiration from Italian nineteenth century arcaded *gallerias*, he provided America with its first multi-level fully air-conditioned covered shopping precinct. In each of these and later schemes the shops have been conceived as the centre piece of a subsequent development of flats, offices and other buildings intended, eventually, to create a powerful regional focus and thus help contract and give shape to suburban sprawl.

Gruen has developed some of the ideas first evolved in the planning of these centres in many large scale proposals for city centre revitalisation. One of his best known plans, for Forth Worth, Texas—appropriately de-

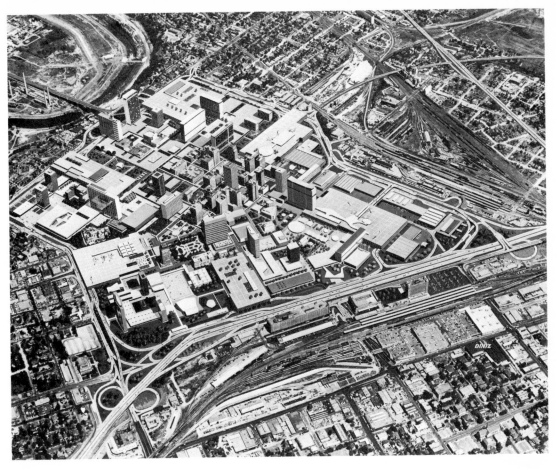

24. Victor Gruen: Model of Fort Worth Development

scribed by Gruen in terms of a fortification against the invading motor car—envisages a road system of three concentric motorways, the inner one circumscribing a traffic-free square mile commercial and business area serviced by underground tunnels. Motorists bound for the centre would park either off the outer roads in car parks linked to it by rapid public transport or off the inner road in multi-storey car parks and continue their journey by moving pavement or in the small electric buses which would be the only vehicles permitted to circulate within the pedestrian area. There would be parking provision for 60,000 cars and no building in the centre would be more than a three minute walk from car park, taxi or bus station. Elimination of traffic from the centre would be celebrated by alterations to the original gridiron street pattern: narrowing

some streets to create intimate passages, widening some into landscaped squares, covering others to form arcades, and providing fountains, flowerbeds, trees, kiosks, seats and open air cafes throughout.

Although the Forth Worth scheme has not been implemented, it has had an undoubted influence on planners throughout America and many of its underlying principles have since been employed on a smaller scale, by Gruen himself, in the development (1956–62) of the Midtown Plaza, Rochester, New York. This development contains shops, offices, art galleries, play areas, a hotel and a frequently used auditorium for public meetings and events and is served by basement service roads, a three-storeyed underground car park and a bus terminus. Its centre consists of entirely traffic-free and air-conditioned pedestrian areas, roofed over but pierced with skylights. The first completed development of its type in

America and a place of pilgrimage for study groups and planners from home and abroad, it is attracting increasing numbers of people into the centre of Rochester and seeming, also, to have a revitalising effect on neighbouring areas.

Gruen has also designed planning projects for Boston, Massachusetts; Fresno, California; Kalamazoo, Michigan; Green Bay, Wisconsin; and St Petersburg, Florida. He was born in Vienna where he studied under Peter Behrens and, on entering private practice, designed commercial and residential developments in Austria, Czechoslovakia and Germany. He settled in the U.S.A. in 1938 and became a naturalised American in 1943. His books, which both describe some of his planning projects and the theories and convictions on which they were based, are:

How to Live with your Architect (1950).
Shopping Towns, U.S.A. (with Larry Smith) (1960).
The Heart of our Cities (The Urban Crisis: Diagnosis and Cure) (1964).

H

HAMPSTEAD GARDEN SUBURB

Instigated by Henrietta Barnet, Hampstead Garden Suburb (1903) developed from her involvement with the founders of the National Trust (q.v.) in a campaign to extend Hampstead Heath and from her social work in the East End of London at Toynbee Hall. There she had endeavoured to enhance the living conditions of the working classes by importing culture and art. At Hampstead the aim was to provide an exemplary and more fundamental solution to the housing problem by building homes for working people 'within a 2d fare of Central London' in an environment which, by its harmonious combination of buildings and nature, would itself constitute an uplifting work of art. Thus far the influence of Port Sunlight (q.v.) and Bournville (q.v.) was apparent and acknowledged. But the founders of Hampstead Garden Suburb also set out to challenge the very nature of the conventional suburb itself; by providing a wide diversity of house types, they hoped to create a mixed community and to break down class barriers.

Although the early house prices ranged from £425 to £3,500, this large social objective was never achieved. Houses for the affluent were built much more rapidly than those for the poor and the consequent inflation in values meant that the suburb soon became largely the middle class enclave it remains today.

Environmentally, however, the aim of its planners, Parker (q.v.) and Unwin (q.v.), were fully realised. Among its innovations are the hierarchical road system, in which road width and length are determined by function and use, and the recurring use of the close or cul-de-sac which, for sanitary reasons, had been banished from Victorian housing layouts by earlier bye-law legislation. Both were permitted by the Hampstead Garden Suburb Act of 1906. They reduced road costs and enabled the excessive road widths and resulting visual monotony of earlier suburbs to be replaced by intimate and domestic enclosures and a more pictorial grouping of buildings.

These contrast with the more open layout of the larger houses near the Heath Extension and with the imposing Central Square which, dominated by the two churches by Luytens, is sited at one of the highest points in the suburb and contains the main social buildings. Flowering trees, vegetation and hedges are everywhere in public, private and communal greens and gardens. The mixture is a characteristically English blend of Beaux Arts formalism and a picturesque informality showing the influence of Camillo Sitte (q.v.).

The building of the suburb was accompanied by widespread publicity and it soon gained an international reputation. Mumford (q.v.) has said: 'It paved the way for further innovations by Ernest May in Frankfurt . . . and by Wright and Stein (q.v.) in the United States'. More than any other scheme it popularised the garden suburb idea and by 1914 at least 52 such schemes had been started or completed. In the public mind the concept had come to symbolise town planning.

FURTHER READING
Mumford, Lewis (1961). *The City in History.*
Creese, Walter J. (1966). *The Search for Environment. (The Garden City Before and After)*

HARD SHOULDER
An almost continuous lane alongside a motorway, (q.v.) unmetalled but sufficient to bear the weight of vehicles, for use in emergency.

HAUSSMANN, 1809–91
Baron Georges Haussmann was Prefect of the Seine from 1853 to 1870. During that time he was largely instrumental in regularising—his word—the chaotic consequences of population and social growth within the 'closed' city of Paris.

He has been described as 'Attila of the straight line' and his plans for broad straight streets have been attributed to his desire to comply with Napoleon III's wish to destroy the old street pattern of Paris and render it easy for the police to discipline and control.

Haussmann's plan and strategy, in addition to providing the celebrated water and sewage systems, was the first to consider Paris *as a whole*. Previous plans had sought simply to re-order sections of the city. His plan created great new 'arteries' to improve circulation, and embodied the notion of openspace and 'verdured space'. His surgery certainly had defects; he destroyed irrevocably the tightly woven and diversified fabric of the Ile de la Cité. But it had positive benefits. Within the network of traffic streets he created a system of planted areas, promenades, squares, public gardens and suburban parks.

By this it is sometimes claimed that Haussmann's planning philosophy was determined by two ideas, circulation and respiration; the one shown in the new road pattern, the other in the 'open space' provision.

FURTHER READING
Choay, Françoise (1969) *The Modern City: Planning in the 19th Century.*
Hiorns, Frederick (1956). *Town Building in History.*

HIGH RISE BUILDING
Simply, multi-storey buildings more than four storeys high. For most people this means flats or offices in point blocks or slab blocks.

In housing there is a common misunderstanding that high rise and high density (q.v.) are synonymous. Whilst they often are, it is not necessarily so. High densities can be achieved with three and four storey housing. Equally, a single point block in parkland may produce no greater density (q.v.) than many two storey dwellings spread over the ground (*see also* Roehampton).

FURTHER READING
Jensen, Rolf (1966). *High Density Living.*

HIPPODAMUS
The father of town planning, born in Miletus (q.v.) probably about 500 B.C. He is credited with introducing broad streets crossing each other at right angles, replacing the crooked narrow lanes common in the rest of Greece. It is said that the main crossing point became the natural point for the agora and its splendid buildings.

Though his repute is probably somewhat overstated Hippodamus certainly stood for the idea of method, of predetermined planning as against the whims of fancy. His sense of order and concern for a disciplined plan was matched by a belief in the importance of the disposition and design of housing. This is probably seen best at Selinus, a smaller, colonial version of Miletus (q.v.).

FURTHER READING
Hiorns, Frederick (1956). *Town Building in History*.
Wycherley, R. E. (1949). *How the Greeks Built Cities*.

HISTORIC BUILDINGS BUREAU

The Bureau is a government sponsored body under the Department of the Environment. It offers a service to possible purchasers or tenants by providing information on historic buildings (i.e. those statutorily 'listed') in England. With the agreement of the owner and only after it has been handled by an estate agent for at least two months it circulates information to a number of bodies who might be interested.

ADDRESS
Historic Buildings Bureau, 2, Marsham Street, London, S.W.1.

HISTORIC BUILDINGS COUNCIL(S)

These councils (for England, Scotland and Wales) were set up by the Historic Buildings and Ancient Monuments Act 1953 as advisory bodies and are concerned with 'buildings of *outstanding* historic or architectural interest'.

Their advisory role includes giving guidance to the Secretary for the Environment, through the Minister for Local Government and Development on: acquisition, the acceptance as gifts and the disposal of such outstanding buildings; grants towards the acquisition of such buildings by local authorities or the National Trust; grants towards the repair and maintenance of such outstanding buildings and their general state; the listing of buildings; new uses for historic buildings (through the Historic Buildings Bureau) (q.v.).

They also run Town Schemes (q.v.).

ADDRESSES
Historic Buildings Council, Sanctuary Buildings, Great Smith Street, London, S.W.1.

Historic Buildings Council, Welsh Office, Summit House, Windsor Place, Cardiff.
Historic Buildings Council, Argyle House, Edinburgh, 3.

HISTORIC BUILDINGS TRUST

An organisation to secure the conservation (q.v.) of buildings of architectural or historic interest. This may involve purchase, repair, management or maintenance (or all of them).

The actual organisation may vary. Some trusts are run by individuals or amenity societies (q.v.). Others consist of people representing industrialists, local authorities, voluntary bodies, set up to be the central 'clearing house' for financial aid to those restoring or repairing architecturally or historically important buildings. In some cases the Trust itself may actually acquire, renovate and then lease or sell buildings.

There are a number of such trusts and a typical one might cover a County Council or County Borough area (see Local Government); it might receive some income from the council or councils and some from private sources. Its work would include making surveys, giving grants and commenting on changes to listed buildings (q.v.).

FURTHER READING
Civic Trust (1971). *Financing the Preservation of Old Buildings*.
Civic Trust (1972). *Conservation in Action*.

HOLFORD, William Graham, (Lord), 1907–

Probably the best-known name in British Town Planning today. A Life Peer and Emeritus Professor of Town Planning in the University of London, Holford's career has been distinguished from the very beginning.

Born in Johannesburg in 1907, Holford was trained in the Liverpool School of Architecture under Sir Charles Reilly (q.v.). He won the Rome Scholarship in Architecture in 1930, became a lecturer in Architecture at Liverpool University in 1933 and Lever Professor of Civic Design in the same University in 1936, at the age of 29.

25. High Rise: Development on Pepys Estate for G.L.C.

During this time he designed many government-sponsored industrial estates in the North East, including Team Valley at Gateshead. With the onset of the Second World War he joined Lord Reith's reconstruction secretariat and, in 1943, the Ministry of Town and Country Planning.

Holford prepared the reconstruction plan for the City of London (1946–8), became part-time professor at University College and taught at Harvard. He prepared development plans for Cambridge, Pretoria and Canberra and was the British assessor in the competition for Brasilia. He has been associated with most of the celebrated planning issues of the day, such as the redevelopment of Piccadilly Circus and St Paul's Cathedral Precinct.

He has been concerned with the preservation of historic buildings and is a member of the Historic Buildings Council (q.v.) and is chairman of its committee on Listed Buildings (q.v.).

In 1953 he was President of the Town Planning Institute (now R.T.P.I.) and of the R.I.B.A. (q.v.) in 1960–62. He received the R.I.B.A. Gold Medal for architecture in 1963 and the R.T.P.I. Gold Medal in 1961. Created a Knight Bachelor in 1953, Lord Holford is a part-time member of the Central Electricity Generating Board and is President of the Housing Centre, London.

HOOK

A small village in Hampshire, some 40 miles from London, of significance in the planning world only because it gave its name to a proposed new town for the (then) London County Council.

The planning and design work was conducted between 1958 and 1961 when it was finally abandoned for political reasons. Ironically, it has probably had more influence on new town design even than Cumbernauld, (q.v.) which it resembled, because the energy that might have been poured into its realisation was, instead, directed towards a detailed documentation about its planning philosophy.

The town, designed for 100,000 people would have abandoned the notion of neigh-

bourhood units (q.v.) and instead was designed so that 70 per cent of its population would have been within five minutes' walk of the central area. The plan also featured a linear, elevated town centre, with servicing from beneath. Industry was grouped at opposite ends of the town's distributor road system to maximise use of the roads. Other features of the plan included a series of large balancing lakes and an attempt to achieve a much more balanced population (in age/sex structure) than was then common in New Towns (q.v.).

Among the distinguished planners and architects involved on the plan was Graeme Shankland (q.v.).

FURTHER READING
London County Council (1961). *Hook: the Planning of a New Town.*

HOUSING ASSOCIATIONS AND SOCIETIES

Non profit-making bodies formed by various groups (usually with special tenants in mind) to build new or convert old houses for people to rent unfurnished. Many such organisations have been formed since the late 1950s and their activities are increasing. The two organisations are slightly different:

(i) Housing Associations usually, though not always, provide accommodation for local people who are unable to obtain local authority accommodation for one reason or another: they may be low on a housing list, old or overseas residents. One such Association has provided accommodation for overseas students. Their finance, in the form of grants or loans, comes mostly from local authorities.

(ii) Housing Societies tend to cater for a wider range of people. Their money comes from the Housing Corporation, a government sponsored agency but which receives some money from the Building Societies. Accommodation is let in one of two ways, 'cost-rent' or 'co-ownership'. The 'cost-rent' basis is organised so that the rent covers the cost of a 40-year mortgage repayment plus the cost of keeping the building in good repair. 'Co-ownership' means that tenants are share-holders in a co-operative society, and if they move away they receive a part of the increased value of the accommodation from the time of their first occupation.

The quality of housing provided by either means is often much better than speculative or council housing.

FURTHER READING
Information Booklets from the National Federation of Housing Societies and the Housing Corporation.

ADDRESSES
The National Federation of Building Societies, 86, Strand, London, WC2.
The Housing Corporation, Sloane Square House, London, SW1.

HOWARD, Ebenezer, 1850–1928

A man assured of a place in town planning history by virtue of his evolution of the Garden City idea.

Born in 1850, Howard became a steno-grapher in the City of London. His familiarity with its problems played a considerable part in stimulating him to devise a diagrammatic form of city in his book *Garden Cities of Tomorrow.*

He undoubtedly saw the Garden City as a refuge from the big city. It aimed at combining the social advantages of the city and the health of rural areas.

Although limited in size, the garden city was to be autonomous and incorporate all types of people. Conceived as a circular plan (diagram might be a better word) the city encompassed about 6,000 acres though only about a sixth was for the city proper. With a design popula-tion of 32,000 and a radius of about one half mile the diagram shows a central park, sur-rounded by main public buildings. Beyond them was the housing, then the secondary and primary sectors (factories and farms) and beyond that an inalienable green belt.

Howard's idea was that when the 32,000 began to be exceeded a part would form a new nucleus from which a new city would grow. As time passed a whole system of garden cities

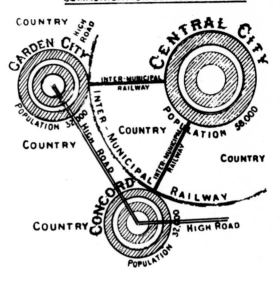

26. Ebenezer Howard: Diagram from his pioneer work on Garden Cities

would evolve around a mother city of about 65,000 people, all interconnected through a system of rapid transit by electric rail.

Howard went on from his theories to col-laborate with Raymond Unwin in developing Letchworth Garden City (q.v.) and then Welwyn (q.v.). Though not many Garden Cities were developed, Howard's ideas and their architectural expression have influenced the whole of suburban England and contri-buted to the success of the post-war New Towns (q.v.) policy.

FURTHER READING
Purdom, C. B. (1963). *The Letchworth Achieve-ment.*
Osborn, F. J. (2nd Ed. 1969). *Green Belt Cities.*

I

I.D.C. (*see* Industrial Development Certificate).

IMPROVEMENT AREAS

The name given to areas predominantly residential in nature which could be marked out by Local Authorities under the 1964 Housing Act. Such designation gave the authority powers over recalcitrant landlords.

These areas were superseded by the stronger provisions of the 1969 Housing Act which authorised local authorities to designate General Improvement Areas (G.I.A.s). Designation is an indication that the Local Authority intends to improve an area as a whole (houses and environment) by using and making available to owners exchequer grants.

Local Authorities encourage owners to take the grants (now up to a maximum of £1,500 per house) and themselves will improve garaging, car parking, landscaping. The schemes may include closing streets and demolishing some houses to make open space. Persuasion is the keynote, compulsory acquisition being used as a last resort. (*See also* Environmental Recovery.)

FURTHER READING
Civic Trust for the North West (1969). *Environmental Recovery at Skelmersdale.*

INDUSTRIAL DEVELOPMENT CERTIFICATE (I.D.C.)

A permit issued by the Department of Trade and Industry giving permission for a new industrial building. It usually relates to a local authority area, does not signify the suitability of a particular site and thus is no guarantee that development will or can take place. (Those decisions are the function of the local planning authority.) Equally no planning permission for an industrial building of more than 10,000 sq. feet in S.E. England and 15,000 sq. ft elsewhere is sufficient without an I.D.C.

It is a negative control and is limited in extent. It does not cover existing buildings, so a company may, on being refused an I.D.C. for a new building, buy an existing building and still create an increase in employment that was not wanted and caused the original refusal of the I.D.C. This is possible because the I.D.C. applies to buildings not employment.

FURTHER READING
Cullingworth, J. B. (3rd Ed. 1969). *Town and Country Planning in England and Wales.*

INDUSTRIAL ESTATE

Usually a large area of land devoted entirely to manufacturing industries and their 'parasite' service industries. The idea of a separated industrial area was a natural reaction to the congestion of factories and houses inherited from the nineteenth century. During the twenties and thirties of this century and since 1945 estates have been established by private and public agencies, the former as speculative developments for profit, the latter as a means of encouraging a town or region's growth.

Under the 1960 Local Employment Act, Industrial Estates Management Corporations were established in England, Scotland and Wales to manage the industrial Estates and factories built under earlier legislation.

INTERMEDIATE AREAS (*see* Assisted Areas).

INTERSECTION

The meeting point of two roads. Most commonly used for roads of motorway (q.v.) or near-motorway standard. *Junction* is used for roads of a lower standard. *Interchange* quite

opposite
27. Interchange

54

specifically describes a system of interconnecting roadways in conjunction with grade separation (q.v.) providing for the interchange of traffic between two or more highways on different levels. An interchange may involve roads at four or even more levels.

J

JACOBS, Jane, 1916–

American author and former associate editor of *Architectural Forum* whose book *the Death and Life of Great American Cities,* published in 1962, crystallized the misgivings of many people about the prevailing orthodoxies of American urban renewal and city planning policies.

In Jane Jacobs, Twilight Areas (q.v.) found their poet, and advocates of orderly disorder their polemicist. The theme of her book is the contrast between how she believes cities actually behave and how orthodox planning theories wish them to behave, between the life and vitality of haphazard inner downtown areas of large American cities (and, by extension, large cities anywhere) and the lifelessness of the carefully planned areas that are built to replace them. Her quarrel is with almost every planning concept propounded or practised this century and her villains are Ebenezer Howard (q.v.) for his Garden City idea, Le Corbusier (q.v.) for his Radiant City dream, and adherents of the American City Beautiful Movement for their predilection for grandiose and separate civic zones, and Lewis Mumford (q.v.), Clarence Stein (q.v.) and all other exponents of dispersal and decentralisation who have criticised congested and growing cities without, she believes, properly understanding the intricate ways in which they function. To describe (and dismiss) their collective ideals she coins the term 'Radiant Garden City Beautiful', while to substantiate her own claims she examines 'ordinary scenes and events' in Greenwich Village (q.v.), and in other inner city areas, where she finds that the characteristics which conventional theory seeks to reduce or eliminate—high density, narrow and congested streets, old buildings and a casual admixture of residential, commercial and industrial uses—are precisely those which, in her view, create the tissue of economic and social relationships which generate city vitality and diversity. She concludes that 'the science of city planning and the art of city design, in real life in real cities, must become the science and art of catalysing and nourishing these close-grained working relationships', and suggests a number of planning and administrative measures which might bring about this change.

The Death and Life of Great American Cities is consistently refreshing, witty and pertinent, and for long after publication it provided a compelling subject for dinner discussion all over American cities. Mumford has described it as 'a mingling of sense and sentimentality, of mature judgements and schoolgirl howlers'. Like most polemic it is passionate, extreme, wilful and selective, but it cannot be ignored. In 1969 Mrs Jacobs extended and developed her attack on current planning practice in *The Economy of Cities* which questioned the conventional assumption that economic growth depends on the further expansion of already large and established institutions, suggesting instead that it results from the many unpredictable, unplanned and small offshoots that break away from them.

FURTHER READING
Mumford, L. (1968). *Home Remedies for Urban Cancer.* Essay in *The Urban Prospect.*

56

K

KAHN, Louis, I, 1901–

American architect noted for his imaginative sequence of plans for the redevelopment of Philadelphia (q.v.), designed intermittently between 1952 and 1961.

The last and most fully visualised plan in this series envisaged a number of overhead expressways entering the city on viaducts, forming an enclosing and monumental wall around its centre and feeding into large circular towers containing car parks in their cores, and hotels, department stores and other facilities at their circumferences. Waterways and reservoirs were placed alongside the expressways, warehouses underneath the viaducts, and shopping centres in the ground floors of the garage towers.

In conception the plan may be thought to be related to Kahn's famous Richards Medical Research Building at the University of Pennsylvania, Philadelphia (1957–61), in which the stair towers and air intake stacks are the most prominent features and, indeed, the determinants of the whole design, for it represented an attempt to give forceful *architectural* expression to the utilitarian elements in the city's structure and to the sort of hierarchical traffic plan which he had designed earlier for the city in 1951. 'I feel the time has come', he wrote in 1960, 'to make the distinction between the viaduct architecture of the car and the architecture of man's activities. . . . Viaduct architecture would encompass an entirely new concept of street movement which distinguished the stop and staccato movement of the bus from the go movement of the car. The areas framing the expressways are like rivers. These rivers need harbours. . . . The harbours are the gigantic gateways expressing the *architecture of stopping*. . . . The terminals of viaduct architecture . . . [the] garages . . . around the centre would present a logical image of protection against the destruction of the city by the motor car.'

Not surprisingly perhaps, Kahn's plan has remained, and is likely to remain, a paper plan.

Highways have been built along the routes he suggested but they are conventional roads. His conception has nevertheless made him the most notable contemporary exponent in America of what has become known as concept planning—that approach to planning which seeks first and foremost to give a meaningful and imageable physical expression to the shape and structure of a town or city.

Born in Russia, Kahn was taken to the U.S.A. at the age of four and graduated in architecture at the University of Pennsylvania in 1924. For much of his career he has worked for Philadelphia City: he has been Consultant Architect to the Housing Authority (1937), the Planning Commission (1946–52 and 1961) and to the Redevelopment Authority (1951–4). He has also been Professor of Architecture at Yale University (1947–57) and at the University of Pennsylvania (1957–   ). His private practice dates from 1934. He was awarded the R.I.B.A. (q.v.) Gold Medal in 1972.

FURTHER READING

Gruen, Victor (1964). *The Heart of Our Cities (The Urban Crisis: Diagnosis and Cure)*.
Scully, Vincent. *Louis I. Kahn* (1962).

KARLSRUHE

A town in the former Grand Duchy of Baden which shows Italian planning principles applied to a new town in the eighteenth century. Created under the direction of an ambitious prince it is fan-shaped and focussed on the palace. Contemporary engravings show the grandiose design, with a large open space between the castle and the town and the main concentric street completing its course in the forest land at the rear of the palace. By means of the radial streets the palace and its tower were meant to be visible from the streets of the town and the countryside.

As Karlsruhe grew beyond its intended

28. Karlsruhe: An 18th-century engraving

population of some 20,000 people it developed an industrial area and suburbs but it takes its place in town planning history as an example of the Renaissance town comprehensively built up on a unified principle of parts related to a whole. It took the idea of the garden at Versailles and built it into a whole town.

FURTHER READING
Hiorns, Frederick (1956). *Town Building in History.*

THE LAND COMMISSION

This was set up by the Land Commission Act 1967 to administer the Act, operate as a land-holding-agency and collect a levy from anyone developing land or selling it to someone else for development.

The object of the whole exercise was two-fold:

(i) To enable a national agency to acquire land and assemble it in such a form as to enable development of a particular sort to occur. The Land Commission was therefore free to make such land available to anyone capable of developing the land in the right way. The price it would pay for such land would be less-than-market-value.

(ii) To equalise the development value (the difference between existing value and the market value) of land sold to the Commission and that sold privately by exacting a 40 per cent levy from the vendor or developer. This money would help finance the commission and the acquisition of further land.

The establishing legislation was extremely complex and in practice the commission was very slow in getting under way. Had it continued there is little doubt it could gradually have acquired substantial areas of the country and (ultimately) all of it. But the concept of the nationalisation of land which it embodied was anathema to the Conservative Party and was abolished soon after their return to power in 1970.

Once again (as in the 1940s) an attempt to harness the (or some of the) profits in land development for the nation and facilitate development in the right places at the right time had failed.

LANE

A longitudinal division of a carriageway intended to accommodate a single line of moving vehicles. It has become a means of increasing the effective use of road space when motorists are encouraged (or directed) to obey a certain lane discipline and not wander over a wider area of road than they need. On motorways it has made possible the restriction of certain types of vehicles (lorries and cars towing trailers) to the two inside lanes.

LETCHWORTH

The first Garden City and first realisation of the ideas put forward by Ebenezer Howard (q.v.) in his *Garden Cities of Tomorrow*.

Howard's book, published in 1898, aroused considerable interest and its thesis was further publicised by the Garden Cities Association which he formed in 1899. But although lectures were given throughout the country, conferences held at Bournville (q.v.) and Port Sunlight (q.v.) and converts made, interest remained largely academic. The idea of creating *de novo* an entire town by private enterprise seemed too utopian.

The Association was, however, determined to demonstrate its practicability. The Garden City Pioneer Company was formed to identify a site and in 1903 it acquired 3,918 acres in Hertfordshire, 35 miles north of London, and commissioned Parker (q.v.) and Unwin (q.v.) to prepare a plan. The plan reflects many of Howard's ideas. The built up area was to occupy only 1,300 acres of the total site, the rest being reserved for an agricultural and recreational 'green belt' (q.v.). Industry is placed near the railway in a separate zone from the residential areas. An informal road layout, radiating from a central Beaux Arts civic and shopping area, creates a series of superblocks which are sometimes penetrated by culs-de-sac, closes and courts. Through roads are never less than 40 feet wide (between front gardens) and their margins are generously planted with trees and

grass. Some have only one species of tree to strengthen their identity. Houses at a maximum density (q.v.) of 12 to the acre are positioned to obtain the sunniest and most pleasant views and set back a minimum distance of 20 feet from the footpaths to ensure privacy. Each has its own garden at back and front. Allotments and children's play areas are also provided. A lavish provision of trees, flowers, foliage and herbage adorns, and sometimes threatenes to submerge, the whole town.

Letchworth has so mellowed with time, and its architectural idiom and visual characteristics have since been so widely imitated and bastardised in innumerable suburban developments, that both the pioneering spirit of those who created it and the planning philosophy that inspired them to do so have been perhaps too often and too easily overlooked. Here for the first time an entirely new and largely self-supporting industrial town, encircled by a green belt, limited in size and designed according to an overall master plan, had been created from scratch. It was an answer to the problem of urban congestion that proved difficult to ignore for ever and it furnished the Town and Country Planning Association (q.v.) and their supporters with a working example of the policy of dispersal, and one which, with Welwyn Garden City (q.v.), they were able to use in their vigorous and eventually successful campaign for a national New Towns (q.v.) policy.

FURTHER READING
Osborn, F. J. and Whittick, Arnold (2nd Ed. 1969). *New Towns: the Answer to Megalopolis*.
Purdom, C. B. (1963). *The Letchworth Achievement*.
Creese, Walter J. (1966). *The Search for Environment (The Garden City Before and After)*.
Ashworth, W. (1954). *The Genesis of Modern British Town Planning*.

LEVEL OF MOTORISATION

A term to describe the number of vehicles per head of population. In 1971 the number of vehicles on British roads was estimated as 15,000,000. Consequently the level of motorisation at that time, assuming a population of 55 million, was 0·27.

FURTHER READING
Drake, James (1969). *Motorways.*

LINEAR CITY
A planned city determined by a main axis (thoroughfare) on both sides of which a development is situated. The term was introduced by a Spanish Engineer, Soria y Mata, in 1882, who recommended the creation of a *Cuidad Lineal* in strips along both sides of a highway 160 feet wide. Part of a linear city was constructed outside Madrid between 1894 and 1896 but after almost three miles had been completed the project was abandoned.

FURTHER READING
Collins, G. (1965). *The Pedestrian and the City.*
Jones, Emrys (1966). *Towns and Cities.*

LINEAR PROGRAMMING
A mathematical language of activities. It describes how these activities use their resources in order to do certain prescribed jobs: it also describes how these activities operate within time and space. The basic description must take the form of a linear algebraic equation, hence the term 'linear programming'. Following its use in wartime and in commercial production centres it has been developed for use in transportation and traffic.

FURTHER READING
Bruton, M. J. (1970). *Introduction to Transportation Planning.*

LISTED BUILDING
A building listed by the Department of the Environment or the Secretary of State for Wales as being of special architectural or historic interest. Once included on the lists a building is afforded a measure of protection against demolition, alteration and neglect.

All buildings built before 1700 which survive in anything like their original form, and most buildings of 1700 to 1840 are listed, while those built between 1840–1939 must be of a definite quality, character or interest. In compiling the lists consideration is given to a building's technological innovation or virtuosity, its association with well-known characters or events, its group value with other buildings and its importance in architectural, planning, social or economic history. The lists classify the buildings in two grades to show their relative importance and are available for inspection at the National Monument Record, the Welsh Office, and at the office of the relevant local authority. Any one may recommend a building for listing.

Legislation requires that anyone wishing to demolish a listed building or to alter it in a way that would affect its character must apply for Listed Building Consent from the appropriate local authority which must advertise and invite comment on the application from various local and national amenity bodies. Local authorities are also empowered to prevent listed buildings from falling into disrepair and may give grants (q.v.) and loans towards their maintenance. Churches belonging to the established church and in ecclesiastical use, and Crown properties (except when held on lease) are exempt from listed building control.

The lists of buildings of architectural or historic interest were completed in 1969, (about 120,000 buildings) and are currently being revised.

FURTHER READING
Ministry of Housing and Local Government. Circulars 53/67 and 61/68.
Ministry of Housing and Local Government. *Protecting Our Historic Buildings: A Guide to Legislation.*
Ward, Pamela (1968). *Conservation and Development.*

LIVERPOOL
The second port of the United Kingdom and a fine Victorian city. But it owes its place in any account of British Planning to the period

from 1962–5 when it was the first major city to appoint a Planning Consultant, Graeme Shankland (q.v.), to prepare plans for the comprehensive redevelopment of its Central Area. Many concepts and techniques that have since become normal were first produced in a series of planning reports. These were presented at regular intervals to the council and general public as opposed to the then usual custom of preparing a masterplan over a two or three year period before divulging its contents.

Hard on the heels of the Central Area plan came the creation of the first really inter-disciplinary city planning department under the leadership of Walter Bor. This department pioneered the idea of 'Structure Plans' (q.v.), subsequently adopted by the Planning Advisory Group (q.v.) and built into the Town and Country Planning Act of 1968. (*See also* Reilly, Charles Herbert.)

FURTHER READING
Bor, Walter and Shankland, Graeme (1965). *Liverpool City Centre Plan.* (for Liverpool Corporation).

LOCAL GOVERNMENT

The collective term we give to the various democratically elected councils that are the means of providing many local services (such as police, ambulance, welfare, education). To make such provision they levy local taxes (rates) and receive additional financial assistance from Central Government (q.v.).

The present pattern of local government has remained substantially unaltered since 1888 but considerable changes will occur in 1974. At present there are a number of different councils, also called 'local authorities'. They are:

County Borough Council. An autonomous, single tier council, responsible for the provision of all services including planning in a large urban area (such as Bristol, Liverpool, Newcastle, etc.).

County Council. A two-tier rural counterpart to the County Borough Council having its total area subdivided into Boroughs, Urban Districts and Rural Districts (which are divided into civil parishes). County Councils have councillors and aldermen, elected to serve an area within a district or borough, and are elected every three years. Among the County Councils responsibilities are education, highways and planning (q.v.) though some aspects of planning may be delegated to the Boroughs or Districts.

Borough, Urban and Rural District Councils are responsible for housing, drainage, local roads, refuse collection, parks and, if given delegated powers (q.v.), planning. Such councils are elected by one third every year.

From 1974 onwards County Boroughs will cease to exist. After many abortive attempts to reform Local Government the Local Government Act of 1972 sets up a new structure. The whole country is to be governed by a two part system. For the extensive country areas there will be the traditional County Councils but with modified powers and divided into districts. For extensive urban areas or conurbations there are to be Metropolitan Counties also subdivided into districts.

Although it is still not precisely clear who will do what in planning terms, because so much is being left to the respective authorities to work out between them, the broad picture is this:

Structure Plans (q.v.) will be prepared by the counties and they will have control over strategy and long term planning.

Local Plans (q.v.) for the most part will be prepared by the districts (although the county will have to be consulted) and it is at district level that most development control (q.v.) will be exercised.

FURTHER READING
Central Office of Information (Annual). *Britain: An Official Handbook.*
Clarke, John J. (20th Ed. 1969). *Outline of Local Government of the U.K.*

LOCAL PLAN

The plan made by the local planning authority (q.v.) (in future likely to be the District Council) for an area within the broad policy of the Structure Plan (q.v.). The plan is sufficiently detailed to show what sort of development will be permitted and where. The local plan may be one of a number of different types, such as a town centre plan, a conservation plan or an action area plan.

The really significant thing about the local plan is that it is not subject to the approval of the Secretary of State but, after suitable public inquiry (q.v.), may be approved locally.

FURTHER READING
M.H.L.G. 1970. *Development Plans: A Manual on Form and Content.*

LOCAL PLANNING AUTHORITY
The name given to those types of local councils given the task under the Town and Country Planning Acts of preparing and administering Development Plans (q.v.). From 1947 to the present (and until the enactment of local government (q.v.) reform) all the County Councils and County Borough Councils in England and Wales were designated Local Planning Authorities. For purposes of Development Control (q.v.) a Planning Authority may delegate some of its powers to district councils (q.v.). After 1974 County Councils (q.v.) and District Councils (q.v.) will be Local Planning Authorities (*see also* Local Government).

FURTHER READING
Central Office of Information (1968). *Town and Country Planning in Britain.*

LOS ANGELES
Los Angeles, the largest city in California and the third largest in the U.S.A., has acquired an almost mythological status. The name derived from it, Angeleno, is not used, like Londoner or Mancunian merely to describe an inhabitant. It has come to be applied as well, most often as a term of abuse, to all those who seem by their policies, writings or views, to endorse or support the planning philosophy or life-style that the city has come to symbolise.

For LA (as it is also known) is unique among cities in that its development has kept pace with the increasing mobility of society. It was not consciously planned at any one stage to accommodate any projected number of motor cars, nor, like most other cities, has it been forced to adapt itself to an increasing car ownership. It has simply grown up with the car. As more road space has been required so has it been made available, until one third of the 70 square mile Los Angeles area and two thirds of its centre are now occupied by elevated expressways, vast and multi-level intersections, streets, garages and car parks. 'It is as though London stretched unbroken from St Albans to Southend in a tangle of ten-lane four deck super parkways, hamburger stands, topless drugstores, hippie hideouts, Hiltons drive-in mortuaries, temples of obscure and extraordinary religions, sinless joy and joyless sin, restaurants built to resemble bowler hats, insurance offices built to resemble Babylon, all shrouded below the famous blanket of acrid and corroding smog.' (James Cameron).

From this description alone, beginning dismissively but seeming to become half enamoured of the things described, one can sense the peculiar fascination that Los Angeles seems to hold. While native Angelenos speed oblivious on the freeways from private detached home to surfing beach or city centre parking lot, planners hotly debate its merits and demerits. It is seen, on the one hand, as the archetypal regional city fulfilling the universal dream of speed, freedom and personal mobility, allowing each individual to pursue his chosen mode of life without any but selected social contacts and, on the other, as a nightmarish sprawling anti-city, peopled by a rootless and lonely crowd, in which all the rich multifarious and interdependent functions of the traditional city have been eliminated by and subordinated to the means of mass transport. Somewhere in the middle are those for whom Los Angeles is neither a warning of things to come nor a model for future cities, but rather a unique and unrepeatable creation which evolved from a unique set of circumstances and which can be appreciated only by discarding each and every preconception of what a city should or should not be.

FURTHER READING
Banham, Reyner (1971). *Los Angeles.*
Fuller, R. Buckminster (1970). *Utopia or Oblivion.*

29. Low Rise: Admiral's Way, Andover

LOW RISE BUILDING

Two and three storey buildings, usually for housing. This phrase is used to contrast with High Rise Building (q.v.). The typical appearance of a development using low rise building is of tight urban quality with long low blocks grouped around squares or at right-angles to major roads. Contrary to popular belief it is possible to achieve quite high densities (q.v.), as much as 50–60 persons to the acre.

M

MILETUS

A seventh century B.C. city that exerted tremendous influence over the surrounding area and indeed much of Ancient Greece and 200 years later was to become probably the first city to be built on a regularised chessboard pattern.

Added to this systematic plan was a dignified use of space in the design of the Agora or forum. This disciplined, ordered city was all the more remarkable for its being built on a peninsular site.

FURTHER READING
Hiorns, Frederick R. (1956). *Town Building in History.*
Wycherley, R. E. (1949). *How the Greeks built Cities.*

MOTORWAY

A road reserved for certain classes of motor traffic only. As used in the U.K. the term also signifies a road with no direct access to property and with grade-separated intersections throughout.

30. Lewis Mumford

Urban Motorway is a motorway in an urban area and often has quite distinct characteristics such as extensive elevated sections, a reduced hard shoulder (q.v.) safety barriers on all sides and high-mast lighting.

FURTHER READING
Drake James (1969). *Motorways*.
British Road Federation (1956). *Urban Motorways*.

MUMFORD, Lewis, 1895–

An influential American writer on planning and sociology.

Mumford was born in Flushing, Long Island, New York, and trained at the City College of New York, Columbia University and the New School of Social Research. In his early days he hoped to become an electrical engineer or playwright but his discovery in 1915 of the

writings of Patrick Geddes (q.v.) turned him increasingly towards a study of urban civilisation and for the next few years, in his own words, he 'explored the environment further in vocational participation'—in the Dress and Waist Industry, as an assistant at a cement testing laboratory in Pittsburgh, as a radio operator in the U.S. Navy and, in 1920, as acting editor in London of *The Sociological Review*. During these formative years he became actively involved in the movement for urban planning on a regional scale and was a co-founder of the Regional Planning Association of America. His first book on planning, *The Story of Utopias*, was published in 1922.

Throughout his life Mumford has been active in politics, religion, education and philosophy and has described himself as a 'generalist or, if a specialist, then one in the all-inclusive field of social philosophy'. He is a humanist in the tradition of Emerson, Melville and Whitman. When writing on planning, he has endeavoured to refer, as far as possible, to places he has known at first hand. He has thus brought to his many studies of urban life a unique blend of erudition, humanity and incisive personal observation.

A recurring theme in Mumford's writings is the need to take 'a long running start in history, in order to solve the problems of today'. Thus in his trilogy, *The Culture of Cities* (1938), *The Condition of Man* (1944) and *The Conduct of Life* (1951), his plea for the recovery of civilisation through the 'moral renewal' of man is preceded by an examination of the way in which man's personality has been shaped throughout history by the communities and organisations he has created. Similarly, *The City in History* (1961) which 'opens with a city that was, symbolically, a world . . . (and) . . . closes with a world that has become, in many respect, a city', seeks to evolve planning principles for the future from a study of the past.

Mumford has acknowledged the influences of Ebenezer Howard (q.v.), Raymond Unwin (q.v.), Barry Parker (q.v.), Patrick Abercrombie (q.v.) and, of course Geddes (q.v.), and, in the tradition of these writers, he has consistently advocated the regional city and the balanced neighbourhood (q.v.) as the solution to the problems of the congested and over-grown city. Any attempt to outline the pro-found influence he himself has exerted would almost inevitably be incomplete, but his impact on the planning of Greenbelt Towns in the U.S.A. and on the post-war reconstruction of Coventry (q.v.) should be mentioned.

He has been professor at Stanford University, Berkeley, the University of Pennsylvania and the Massachusetts Institute of Technology. He has received the Howard Medal and the Gold Medals of both the Royal Institute of British Architects (q.v.) and the Royal Town Planning Institute (q.v.). Apart from the books already described his principal works on planning and related matters are:

Sticks and Stones (1924).
The Brown Decades (1931).
Technics and Civilisation (1934).
City Development (1945).
The Highway and The City (essays) (1963).
The Myth of the Machine (1967).
The Pentagon of Power (1970).
The Urban Prospect (essays) (1968).
Letters of Lewis Mumford and Frederick Osborn (1971).

NATIONAL BUILDING AGENCY
The National Building Agency, set up in 1964 is a limited company, financed initially from government funds. The agency offers advice to clients, contractors, materials, producers and the building professions on the most modern ideas and techniques and brings clients' demands together so that industrialised methods can be more widely used. It has recently begun to take an interest in Environmental Recovery (q.v.) and has acted as an agency for such work for local authorities.

ADDRESS
National Building Agency, N.B.A. House, Arundel Street, London, WC2.

NATIONAL PARKS
Established where substantial areas of country-side are considered to be of such beauty and value that they need to be conserved for the nation. But, unlike National Parks elsewhere in the world, those in Britain are not publicly owned and there is no general right of public access (though many access agreements have been drawn to enable public enjoyment of the parks).

Ten in number, The National Parks of England and Wales are in Northumberland, North Yorkshire Moors, the Lake District and Peak District, Dartmoor, Exmoor, Snowdonia, the Brecon Beacons and the Pembrokeshire coast. They are differently governed, with committees drawn from local planning authori-ties (q.v.). Only the Peak Park has a completely separate Planning Board with its own staff and office.

Much controversy has surrounded the ques-tion of how best to manage the National Parks when the reform of Local Government (q.v.) takes place in 1974. There is obviously room for improvement, but the present system has managed to protect substantial areas of country, with the Countryside Commission (q.v.) keep-ing a close watch on the local committees or boards and providing financial aid to maintain and enhance character and provide facilities for the greater public enjoyment of the Parks.

FURTHER READING
Abraham Harold (1969). *Britain's National Parks.*
Countryside Commission (1968–). Annual Reports.

NATIONAL TRUST
Its full title is 'National Trust for Places of Historic Interest or Natural Beauty'. Founded

in 1895 by Octavia Hill, Sir Robert Hunter and Canon Rawnsley. Their aim was to set up a body of private citizens who would act as trustees for the nation in acquiring and managing land and buildings considered worthy of permanent preservation.

Nowadays the Trust owns about 350,000 acres, and some 200 houses of great architectural or historical importance. The variety of properties is tremendous, ranging from dovecotes to whole mountains or villages. Most of its properties can never be sold or mortgaged or acquired compulsorily without the special agreement of Parliament.

The properties are usually open to the public and are often lived in privately. Where a charge is made for admission, Trust Members can (on production of their membership card) be admitted free of charge.

Administered by a Council (some appointed by public bodies and societies and some elected by members) which delegates its main responsibilities to an executive committee, it is run from London. The Trust is national and independent from government though it does receive help in relief from taxation, grants for repairs and gifts of land and buildings. Over 200,000 people now belong to the Trust whose role is of increasing importance as the conservation of the past is more readily accepted and the value of ownership, maintenance and management more fully understood.

ADDRESSES

National Trust for Places of Historic Interest or Natural Beauty, 42, Queen Ann's Gate, London, S.W.1.

National Trust for Scotland, 5 Charlotte Square, Edinburgh, EH2 4DU.

FURTHER READING

Fedden, Robin (1968). *The Continuing Purpose.*

National Trust (1968). *The Benson Report on the National Trust.*

Ryan, Peter (1969). *The National Trust.*

31. Neighbourhood Unit: Shopping centre in Crawley New Town

NEIGHBOURHOOD UNIT

A concept, dating from America in the 1920s, that towns or cities can be sub-divided into almost self-contained social units. The idea has been variously developed over the years, the term being used at different times to describe 2,500 to 15,000 people. The popular figure is 10,000 people, or that population which may be served by one primary school. Much·has been written about this from Clarence Perry in the 1930s, right down to the last decade. The idea has been used in Russia (Magnetogorsk) on a most rigid basis and was central to the plans for all the early New Towns (q.v.) in the U.K.

In recent years, it has fallen into disrepute as a planning device. Greater personal mobility, the realisation that no physical devices satisfactorily create social cohesion and the thought that people should be able to walk easily into the main shopping and business areas have all contributed to this.

FURTHER READING

Fawcett, C. B. (1944). *A Residential Unit for Town and Country Planning*.

Mann, P. H. (1958). 'The Socially Balanced Neighbourhood', *Town Planning Review*, Vol. 29; No. 2.

Perry, C. A. (1939). *Housing for the Machine Age*.

NEW DELHI

Capital of India designed in 1913 by Sir Edwin Lutyens (with Sir Edward Barker) to supersede the old capital of Calcutta.

In plan the city is shaped like an immense, diamond-shaped parallelogram. A broad, spacious and tree-lined central axis, flanked by water, parkland and parallel avenues, leads from one acute angle up the middle of the diamond to culminate near the centre in a monumental complex of government buildings reached up a gradient. This consists of two Secretariats placed on either side and, beyond them, past a formal court and closing the vista, the former Viceregal Lodge (now the President's Palace). Other avenues, parallel to the central axis, perpendicular to it and parallel with the

sides of the diamond, intersect at *rond-points* and stretch into the distance or are terminated with buildings. Beyond the Government buildings, which are generally held to represent a skilful mixture of Eastern and Western architectural styles, the central axis is continued by a formal rectilinear garden with water and fountains.

The whole plan is the largest and most grandiose expression of Baroque planning principles in the twentieth century.

FURTHER READING

Cullen, Gordon (1961). *Townscape*.

Hussey, Christopher (1950). *The Life of Sir Edwin Lutyens*.

NEW TOWNS

The modern 'New Town' is a direct descendant of the proposals put forward by Ebenezer Howard (q.v.) in the last decade of the nineteenth century. The whole development of a new towns policy in Britain evolved gradually from the first garden cities at Letchworth (q.v.) and Welwyn (q.v.) through the propagandist activities of organisations such as the Town and Country Planning Association (q.v.) and through the plans put forward by Sir Patrick Abercrombie for London in 1943 and 1944.

In 1946 the 'New Towns Act' (q.v.) was passed in Parliament, following closely the recommendations of Lord Reith's New Town Committee which had been set up in October 1945. Under the Act it was the Government's intention to initiate up to 20 new towns. Between 1947–50 work on fourteen commenced, twelve in England and two in Scotland. In 1956 a further Scottish new town was proposed, Cumbernauld. Since then six more new towns have been established, five in England and Wales and a further one in Scotland (see Appendix A) The New Towns Act of 1946 set out government procedure for a national policy of town design. It gave the Minister of Housing and Local Government (then Lord Silkin (q.v.)) and the Secretary of State for Scotland, power to make an order designating any area of land (which included any existing town or other centre of population) as a site for a new town. The Act authorised the creation of independent corporations to design, build and manage (until later handed over to a central agency—the Commission for New Towns) new townships. Initially the Act was passed to create new towns, each with a population range of between 20,000 and 60,000 people, on sites varying in size from 5,500 to 11,000 acres. Fifty million pounds was approved as a consolidated fund to finance the new towns in 1946. Subsequently, with the New Towns Act, 1959, this sum was increased to £400 m. The capital costs for building the new towns is advanced to the corporations from public funds and is repayable over an agreed period out of the income from property. Of the first group of new towns eight were intended to absorb excess population from the Greater London Area.

In the period since 1946 the progress in developing new towns has been in three distinct phases each of which has been reflected in distinctly different physical forms.

Mark I new towns have fairly low densities, are often subdivided into neighbourhood units (q.v.).

Mark II new towns, such as Cumbernauld (q.v.), Skelmersdale and Runcorn are more centralised, reflect the problems of the motor car (either in providing urban motorways or integrated public transport systems) and have higher densities.

Mark III new towns are for much larger populations (up to 500,000). They involve the incorporation of several existing large communities and will see a much greater incidence of private development.

FURTHER READING
Schaffer, Frank (1970). *The New Town Story.*
Osborn, F. J. (2nd Ed. 1969). *Green Belt Cities.*
Osborn, F. J. and Whittick, Arnold (2nd Ed. 1969). *New Towns: the Answer to Megalopolis.*

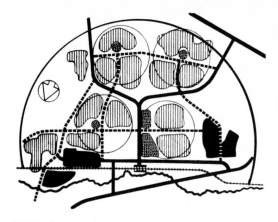

32. New Towns: Diagrammatic plan of Harlow

NEW TOWNS ACT, 1946

This act gave the Minister of Housing and Local Government and the Secretary of State for Scotland power to make an order designating any area of land (which may include any existing town or other centre of population) as the site of a proposed new town, and in 1965 the same power was given to the Secretary of State for Wales. The appropriate minister must consult the local authorities in and around the area about the proposal. Once the site has been designated, the minister appoints a development corporation (consisting of a chairman, a deputy chairman and up to seven other members) to be responsible for the development of the new town.

The development corporations have powers in general (subject to the consent of the appropriate minister) to acquire, by agreement or compulsory purchase, land or property within the designated areas, or, in some cases, land near to or outside those areas, and they may provide houses, flats, commercial and industrial premises, estate roads and other buildings or services essential for the development of the towns. In England and Wales, and in certain cases in Scotland, the development corporations need not obtain planning permission from the local planning authorities.

OPEN SPACE

This is a very loosely used term and is often prefixed by the words 'private' or 'public'.

In general it seems to refer to all land which is used for purposes which do not require many buildings and which enable it to be left substantially in its natural state or to be treated so that it is visually pleasant. There is wide variation as to what is included in the open space category in development plans. Parks, playing fields, cemeteries and allotments are often included with the smaller incidental open spaces around buildings such as hospitals.

Because of these widely differing interpretations of the term standards have differed too over the years. From 1920–40 5 acres per 1,000 population was fairly generally accepted, divided into 3 acres for games and 2 acres for parks. The National Playing Fields Association have suggested 8 acres per 1,000. The Greater London Plan (1951) suggested 10 acres per 1,000, including 3 acres attached to schools and suggests the remaining 7 acres should be distributed as to 1 acre parks, 4 acres public playing fields and 2 acres private playing fields.

FURTHER READING

Best, Robin H. and Coppock, J. T. (2nd Imp. 1965). *The Changing Use of Land in Britain.*

OSBORN, Sir Frederic James, 1885–

Author, planner and propagandist, Sir Frederic Osborn has acquired an international reputation for his sustained and tireless espousal of the principles behind Ebenezer Howard's (q.v.) Garden City idea and for his substantial contribution towards having these principles accepted as integral elements of government planning policy.

Leaving school at the age of 15 and receiving no professional education, Osborn first worked in City offices: for ten years in that of a London housing society. Later, as Secretary/Manager to the Howard Cottage Society in Letchworth, he became interested in the Garden City movement, and in 1918, with Howard, C. B. Purdom, and W. G. Taylor, formed a group for which he wrote *New Towns After the War*, advocating a national policy of planned dispersal, with 100 new towns of moderate size encircled by green belts, as a means of combating urban congestion and sprawl. Osborn then became Estate Manager (1919–36) at Welwyn Garden City (q.v.) of which, with Howard and others, he was co-founder, and an active participant in its social and cultural life.

On retiring as estate manager, Osborn used his authority and unequalled experience to renew and extend the campaign for a national new towns policy. In various capacities, as broadcaster and lecturer, as Chairman of the Town and Country Planning Association (q.v.), as adviser to Lord Reith when Minister of Works and Buildings, in his successful efforts to persuade Churchill's war-time government to accept the main recommendations of the Barlow Report (q.v.), and as member of government and party committees, he was probably more responsible than any one other person for bringing the New Towns Act 1946 (q.v.) on to the statute book. His *Green Belt Cities* (1946; reissued 1969), an account of the Letchworth (q.v.) and Welwyn experiments and a restatement of the essential planning principles underlying them, also contributed to a wider acceptance of the concept of urban dispersal.

Throughout his career, in his books and through innumerable articles and lectures, Osborn has sought to clarify the planning principles (limitation of town size, a degree of economic and social sufficiency, public ownership of land etc.), which distinguish the garden city (or new town) from the 'garden suburb' with which, because of similar visual characteristics, it has often, and sometimes seemingly wilfully, been confused. The title *Green Belt Cities* is in itself part of this attempt.

Sir Frederic has lectured and acted as consultant in the U.S.A., U.S.S.R., Japan and many other countries. He is an Honorary Member of the Royal Town Planning Institute (Gold Medal 1963) and of the American Institute of Planners and received the Silver Medal of the American Society of Planning Officials in 1960. He was Honorary Treasurer and on the Bureau of the International Federation for Housing and Planning from 1944–61, and is now Vice-President; and was knighted in 1956. In addition to the books mentioned and various pamphlets, his publications include: *The New Towns: Answer to Megalopolis* (with Arnold Whittick 1963 and 1969), *Letters of Lewis Mumford and Frederic Osborn* (1971) and *Can Man Plan? and other Verses* (1959).

OVERSPILL

When for any one or more reasons, re-development of an existing residential or industrial area takes place, the resulting new development is rarely able to provide as much accommodation as the former development. This may of course be due to a wish to change the pattern of land use. But even where the pattern of use remains largely unaltered it still occurs. This is due to the need to provide greater land areas for ancillary uses now considered to be socially or functionally essential or desirable. Thus in housing areas, schools, clinics, open spaces etc. are all included at a much greater acreage per head of population than before. In industrial areas, storage, service roads, parking areas, recreation areas have the same effect.

The ultimate outcome, either between one part of a city and another or between a whole city and its surrounding countryside is a surplus of people or activities greater than it can accommodate. This surplus is known as overspill.

Overspill is often quite deliberately planned for with the object of relieving over-crowding or congestion. Catering for such overspill has produced the need for New Towns (q.v.) and the development of existing smaller towns (see also Town Development).

FURTHER READING
Cullingworth, J. B. (3rd Ed. 1970). *Town and Country Planning in England and Wales.*
Self, Peter (2nd Ed. 1961). *Cities in Flood.*
Storm, Michael (1965). *Urban Growth in Britain.*

OWNER-OCCUPIER

Literally, a person who owns a house and lives in it. At a time when both major political parties are encouraging the creation of a home-owning democracy, about 50 per cent of the households in the U.K. are headed by someone who owns his own house and lives in it. In planning and housing the owner-occupier can be both a blessing and a stumbling block. For example, owner-occupation may ensure a high standard of care and maintenance in a particular area, but it may be the means of frustrating change that would be in the interests of the community as a whole. In General Improvements Areas (q.v.) owner occupiers can be the means of securing or preventing a genuine programme of rehabilitation (q.v.).

P

PARKER, Barry, 1867–1947

Although Parker's name is usually associated with Raymond Unwin (q.v.), with whom he worked in partnership at New Earswick near York, Letchworth (q.v.) and Hampstead Garden Suburb (q.v.), his achievements as planner and architect in his own right were considerable.

The largest and most notable design after the partnership had been dissolved, was the plan for a satellite town (q.v.) outside Manchester at Wythenshawe (1927–41), the first local authority experiment in decentralisation in the country and, with Knowsley and Speke near Liverpool (q.v.) one of the very few municipal developments to anticipate the recommendations of the Barlow Report (q.v.). Although Wythenshawe was planned to have too little industry to be a garden suburb, and although its envisaged population of 80,000 to 100,000 was more than twice that prescribed for garden cities by Ebenezer Howard (q.v.), it was designed largely along garden city lines with an agricultural green belt, generous allocation of open space within the built up area, and architectural characteristics, layouts and ambience that recall both Letchworth and Hampstead. Parker did introduce one distinctive innovation however—the Parkway, which was probably inspired by the Chicago and New York parkway systems and was the first in Britain. Houses along Princess Parkway, an arterial road leading out of Manchester, were set back 150 feet from the carriageway behind tree- and shrub-planted swathes of parkland which were intended to act as noise buffers, to create attractive pedestrian areas and to provide both residents and motorists with more pleasant views than could usually be obtained along most ribbon-developed main roads. Although the parkway probably had its source in the expense of building the alternative, a ring road (q.v.), Parker was to develop the concept in his writings, arguing its superiority in modern traffic conditions to concentric road systems and envisaging clusters of towns linked by freeways running through belts of parkland.

Born at Chesterfield, Parker received his training at art schools in Derby and Kensington, London, and started his working life (1887) in the drawing offices of an interior decorator in Altrincham near Manchester. He entered private practice as an architect at Buxton in 1895 and was joined a year later by Unwin in a partnership that lasted until 1914. After that date, and as he increasingly became an international figure, he was employed as consultant to many projects including a civic centre at Oporto in Portugal and a garden suburb at Sao Paulo in Brazil.

In addition to numerous articles and lectures, his writings include:

The Art of Building a Home (1901). (With Unwin).
Town Planning (1907).
Highways, Parkways and Freeways (1937).

PARTICIPATION

One of the major criticisms of the planning process in Britain from 1947 to about 1965 was that people for whom plans were made were not involved in their preparation. Gradually a lobby (fostered by such bodies as the Civic Trust (q.v.)) began to build up for greater public involvement in planning.

Recognition of this lobby resulted in a much greater willingness on the part of local planning authorities to publicise their proposals before making decisions. From about 1964 onwards, draft plans or discussion documents began to appear. Finally in the 1968 Town and Country Planning Act the public was given certain statutory rights.

Section 3(1) of the Act states:

When preparing a structure plan (q.v.) for their area and before finally determining its content for submission to the Minister, the local planning authority shall take such steps as will in their opinion secure:
(a) that adequate publicity is given in their area to the report of the survey under Section 1 above and to the matters which they propose to include in the plan;
(b) that persons who may be expected to desire an opportunity to make representations to the authority with respect to those matters are made aware that they are entitled to an opportunity of doing so; and
(c) that such persons are given an adequate opportunity of making such representations; and the authority shall consider any representations made to them within the prescribed period.

Section 7(1) contains similar provisions for local plans.

In March of 1968, whilst the Planning Act was still passing through Parliament a committee under the chairmanship of the late Arthur Skeffington M.P. (the Parliamentary Secretary at the Ministry of Housing and Local Government) was set up 'to consider and report on the best methods, including publicity, of securing the participation of the public at the formative stage in the making of development plans for their area'. The committee produced its own definition of participation: 'the act of sharing in the formulation of policies and proposals'.

The report was received by Government and eventually a circular appeared endorsing the principle of participation but leaving the method to the Local Planning Authority (q.v.), thereby neither rejecting nor adopting the Skeffington Committee's Recommendations.

For many people the greatest disappointment was that the terms of reference of the committee precluded it from considering public participation in development control (q.v.).

FURTHER READING

Hill, Dilys M. (1970). *Participating in Local Affairs.*

Ministry of Housing and Local Government: Committee on Public Participation in Planning (1969). *People and Planning.*

PASSENGER CAR UNIT

This term enables the capacity of a highway, or the volume of a stream of traffic, to be expressed in terms of a single number which is independent of the type of vehicles in a traffic stream. It allows for the different effect of various types of vehicle by considering them in terms of the equivalent number of passenger cars. The equivalents may vary but the following values are common:

Private cars and light vans	1·0	p.c.u.
motorcycles	0·75	,,
medium and heavy goods vehicles	2·00	,,
buses and coaches	3·00	,,

PAXTON, Joseph, 1803–65

A farmer's son and landscape architect who was for much of his life head gardener and land agent to the Sixth Duke of Devonshire at Chatsworth, Paxton is world famous for his iron and glass Crystal Palace (1851), which was larger than any building ever previously built and the first to consist entirely of mass-produced and standardised prefabricated parts. Although it had little immediate influence, it prefigured changes in architectural practice and the building industry that were to change the face of towns throughout the world.

Scarcely less versatile and bold in his numerous landscaping and planning projects, Paxton, in his layout for Birkenhead Park (1843), set a new standard for town parks in being the first to reflect contemporary urban housing conditions by including areas specifically set aside for recreation and sport. Its independent circulation systems for traffic and pedestrians had been employed in public parks before, but never so comprehensively. Both features were to influence the American landscape architect Frederick Olmstead, particularly in his design for Central Park, New York.

As an M.P. Paxton advocated a number of improvement schemes for London, the most notable of which were the Victoria Embankment (1864–70), which incorporated a new sewer underneath gardens and a spacious Thameside street between Westminster and Blackfriars Bridge, and his proposal for an eleven mile long arcade, The Great Victorian Way, encircling central London and linking all the main railway termini. Similar in style to the Crystal Palace, it was to be lined with shops and houses, used exclusively by pedestrians except for evening and early morning service vehicles, and to have four railway lines, covered in and raised on two levels above the ground, running on each side. No one point on the circuit was to be further than fifteen minutes by train from any other. Although it was never built, the logic behind its conception has since been reflected in the construction of the Underground Inner Circle line. The partial segregation of traffic and pedestrians was well in advance of its time.

opposite
Joseph Paxton
33 & 34. Birkenhead Park, as planned and today

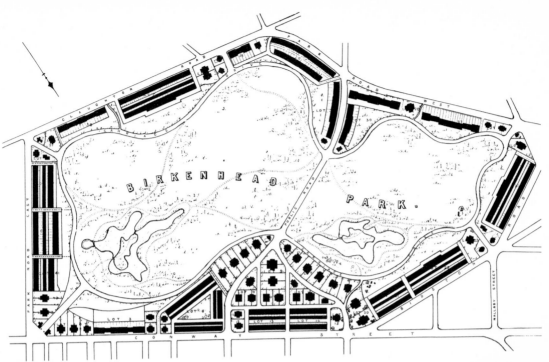

FURTHER READING

Chadwick, G. F. (1961). *The Works of Sir Joseph Paxton.*

Chadwick, G. F. (1966). *The Park and the Town.*

PHILADELPHIA

has a double interest for students of planning. Laid out in 1682 by Thomas Holme to capture the vision of William Penn, it came within that period when the ideas of Vitruvius (q.v.) were being so faithfully followed in Europe. It is not surprising that the plan took a chessboard pattern, with the two main cross roads meeting in an open square that formed the civic centre.

The whole city conceived of by Penn is now almost coincident with the area considered as the city centre.

Its rebirth, under the inspired leadership of Edmund Bacon (q.v.), has been a remarkable planning and development exercise unparalleled elsewhere in the U.S.A. It is today one of the most and best planned of all large American cities. Several exciting projects have been completed within a comprehensive Master Plan.

The first of these schemes was Penn Centre and opposite is the Market East Plaza. This is five blocks long and one block wide. In it are offices, three levels of shopping, a bus terminus, a car park and, at a level to connect with Penn Centre, a raised pedestrian walkway.

Almost every aspect of modern city planning is reflected in Philadelphia. Its Levittown suburban residential community has a major out-of-town shopping centre (see Regional Shopping Centre). As an example of high quality landscape motorways the Schuykhill Parkway is excellent.

Society Hill, a run-down eighteenth-century areas, was rehabilitated until it became something of a status address.

FURTHER READING

Bacon, Edmund N. (1967). *Design of Cities.*

Johnson-Marshall, Percy (1966). *Rebuilding Cities.*

PHOTOGRAMMETRY

A photographic technique used to obtain reliable measurements in order to obtain the geometrical characteristics of an object or a land mass. It is a technique used primarily in topographical mapping. A form of *terrestrial* photogrammetry was introduced as early as 1850 by a Frenchman Aimé Laussedat but within the decade the first experiments in aerial photography took place. Today, the introduction of highly sophisticated electronic aids and extremely wide-angle lenses has increased the scope of photogrammetry both in its aerial usefulness and for ground object surveys. For aerial mapping work over uneven ground a form of double-image (stereoscopic) photogrammetry is used.

PLANNER

Planner is a very widely used (and misused) word. It has no specific legal definition. There are economic planners, traffic planners, regional planners and many more. They are not even necessarily professionally or technically trained. 'Planner', in the local newspaper, may refer to ministry official, local government planning officer, member of parliament or local councillor.

To be a little more specific, however, within the context of land planning the planner is generally taken to be the man who has to cover the whole range of social, economic and physical factors which make up the context of life and who tries to make preparations for its future demands.

A more specific definition is that of 'Chartered Town Planner', the designation of Fellows and Members of the Royal Town Planning Institute (q.v.).

PLANNING

Can mean different things to different people. In its broadest sense it may be said to be the practice of trying to so organise resources that a desired objective is achieved (usually sometime in the future). For some that means simply trying to anticipate the natural trends of society and is known as 'Trend' planning. For others it means defining goals or objectives and then devising policies for achieving those goals, which may mean revising or diverting trends.

A number of adjectives have come to be added to the word. *Advocacy* planning emerged first in the U.S.A. and describes the practice of professional planners voluntarily helping underprivileged sections of society to give expressions to their hopes for a better environment. *Corporate* Planning is the idea, gaining favour in Britain at the present time, of seeing all aspects of public administration as a planning process. *Systems* planning, widely misunderstood, is the idea of using various methodology. Its more responsible proponents the physical planning process a rational methodology. Its more responsible proponants have never declared it a substitute for creative organisational and administrative design, though some people have.

FURTHER READING

Cullingworth, J. B., (3rd Ed. 1969). *Town and Country Planning in England and Wales.*

McLoughlin, J. B., (1969). *Urban and Regional Planning. A Systems Approach.*

Petersen, William (1966). 'On some meanings of "planning",' *Journal of the American Institute of Planners*, Vol. 32.

PLANNING ADVISORY GROUP REPORT (P.A.G. REPORT)

The proper title for this report, published in 1965 is *The Future of Development Plans.* It was produced by a committee of planners and administrators drawn from central and local government, collectively known as the Planning Advisory Group (hence P.A.G.).

Many of their recommendations, about plan types and the need for the responsible Minister to concern himself only with broad principles and strategies were incorporated into the Town and Country Planning Act 1968. It was in the P.A.G. Report that the idea of Structure Plans (q.v.) first saw the light of day.

PLANNING APPEAL

Similar to Planning Inquiry (q.v.), but usually stemming from a Local Planning Authority's refusal to permit some development, or failure to make a decision within the legally prescribed time limit of two months.

The planning applicant then appeals to the Secretary of State to hold an inquiry so that he (the applicant) may appeal against the Local Authority. The Secretary of State may appoint an inspector (as in an Inquiry) or may decide to determine the appeal on receipt of written evidence from both sides, if the parties agree. They often do as it reduces the time needed to reach a decision, which with a full appeal may take many months.

FURTHER READING

Keeble, Lewis (4th Ed. 1969). *Principles and Practice of Town and Country Planning.*

Rose, P. L. and Barnes, M. (2nd Ed. 1970). *Planning Appeals and Inquiries.*

PLANNING APPLICATIONS—Outline and Detail

Anyone intending to 'develop' a piece of land must have permission to do so. Certain developments (as set down in the General Development Order 1950 (q.v.)) are 'deemed' to have permission. In all other cases permission has to be sought from the Local Planning Authority (q.v.).

The applicant need not own the land nor have any legal interest in it. To avoid unnecessary detailed work an applicant may test the attitude of the local authority by making an 'outline' application, on the appropriate form supplied by the authority. Outline planning application seeks permission from the planning authority to development in principle—e.g. the local planning authority may give permission for 'housing' or 'industry' or a 'fish and chip shop' —without agreeing any form or density of development. Permission may be granted subject to subsequent approval by the local planning authority of any matters relating to siting, design and external appearance. Once granted the local planning authority is committed to allowing the proposed development in some form or other, unless it chooses to revoke the permission when compensation has to be paid. It is such a costly process that there have not been many revocations.

SCOTLAND

NORTHERN

YORKSHIRE
AND
HUMBERSIDE

NORTH
WEST

WALES
and
Monmouthshire

EAST MIDLANDS

WEST MIDLANDS

EAST ANGLIA

SOUTH EAST

SOUTH WEST

Whether following an outline application or not, a full application has to be made and granted before work may begin. The local authority may (i) grant permission unconditionally (ii) subject to conditions or (iii) refuse. Any conditions attached have to be reasonable.

In the event of refusal or if conditions seem unreasonable the applicant may appeal (within one month) to the Secretary of State for the Environment, who may reverse the decision, confirm it, add further conditions or even (where permission has been given conditionally) refuse it. In practical terms the Secretary of State's decision is final.

When a planning application is made it has to be acknowledged and if the Local Planning Authority gives no decision in writing within two months, the application is deemed refused and appeal may be made to the Secretary of State, as above. The two month period may be extended by mutual consent.

FURTHER READING

Central Office of Information (1968). *Town and Country Planning in Britain.*

Keeble, Lewis (4th Ed. 1969). *Principles and Practice of Town and Country Planning.*

PLANNING COUNCILS AND BOARDS [ECONOMIC]

In 1965 a system of regional councils and boards was set up in Great Britain. The purpose is to provide effective machinery for regional economic planning. The planning councils consist of about 25–30 part-time members, widely experienced in each area. Having no executive powers, the councils assist in the formation of regional plans and advise on implementation. They also comment on the implications of national policies.

The Planning Boards consist of civil servants representing the main Government Departments concerned with aspects of regional planning in their respective areas. Their task is to prepare draft plans for the region and co-ordinate the economic work of the government departments.

opposite
35. Planning Council Regions

FURTHER READING

Department of Economic Affairs (2nd Ed. 1968). *Economic Planning in the Regions.*

PLANNING INQUIRY

A quasi-legal hearing of the various arguments for and against a Planning Authority's proposals.

The Inquiry was, until the 1968 Planning Act, always held on behalf of the Minister responsible for planning, by an appointed Inspector, usually a trained architect, surveyor, engineer or planner. Under the 1968 Act an inspector may be appointed by a local planning authority to hear objections to a Local Plan (q.v.) though the Minister may appoint someone and still has to for inquiries into Structure Plans (q.v.).

Although the Inquiry is not strictly a legal proceeding, it often has all the appearance of such. But witnesses at the inquiry do not require legal representation. Statements that witnesses will make are exchanged beforehand but there is an opportunity for cross-examination. Planning Inquiries can last weeks and even (though rarely) months.

FURTHER READING
(See Planning Appeal.)

PLANNING OFFICER

Each of the local planning authorities has by law to have a planning officer. In the early years of planning legislation (the 1950s) it was common to combine this role with the engineer or surveyor. County Councils soon began to establish separate departments but County Boroughs retained the dual role for some time; only in the last decade (1961–71) have the larger county boroughs appointed a separate planning officer and the smaller ones often still do not do so.

The planning officer has control of a department and is responsible to a committee for the preparation of plans in accordance with the statutory requirements of planning legislation and the supervision of the development control within the provision of the plans. As time has passed his responsibilities have grown more onerous and the increase in population, traffic and leisure time (to mention only three) call for a high degree of skill.

The latest planning legislation (Town and Country Planning Act 1968) will increase the demands on the planning officer, particularly in respect of the work that will have to be done to secure greater public participation (q.v.).

PLOT RATIO

A technique in town planning for defining the density of development of a particular area. It can either be descriptive of an existing situation or a desired level in excess of which development would not be permitted.

Plot ratio is calculated by measuring the total floor area of a building (including wall thicknesses) and relating it to the area of land within the curtilage of the building site. Thus a three storey building covering the whole site on each floor level has a plot ratio of 3 : 1. So has a six storey building covering half the site.

In most post-war central area re-development schemes a plot ratio not in excess of 3·5 : 1 has been sought.

Various factors may determine the desired plot ratio, including architectural mass and traffic generation. Plot ratio as a technique has been heavily criticised but no genuine alternative has been developed.

FURTHER READING
Johnson-Marshall, Percy (1966). *Rebuilding Cities*.

36. Plymouth: General view of City Centre. The historic Barbican area is in top right-hand corner

PLYMOUTH

Plymouth owes its place in the history of planning to two principal reasons:

(i) It is a fine example of a city reshaping itself for the future after calamitous events (in this case devastation in the Second World War). This was inspired by the foresight and energy of the then Lord Mayor, Viscount Astor.

(ii) It is one of the few plans prepared by Sir Patrick Abercrombie (q.v.) to be substantially completed. Abercrombie's partner in preparing the plan was the City Engineer J. Paton Watson who, with tireless determination, adhered faithfully (sometimes too faithfully) to Abercrombie's plan.

Today the city centre shows the unmistakeable signs of a plan that failed to anticipate the motor vehicle and ignored the impact of wind and rain; it is a Beaux Arts plan with wide straight boulevards, lawns and trees. The architecture which lines the streets is largely undistinguished and monotonous. By contrast the Barbican Area, mercifully preserved in much the same state as in its Elizabethan heyday, is full of interest and variety. This latter is interesting in that much of the preservation and restoration has been achieved by the Barbican Association, an Historic Building Trust (q.v.).

PORT SUNLIGHT

Now a part of the Cheshire borough of Bebington, Port Sunlight is a part of the great Unilever Group of Companies. Comprising factories, training centres, Library, Art Gallery and housing for the company's employees, Port Sunlight is renowned for its grace and beauty. It is a

37. Port Sunlight: Typical black and white Tudor-style housing

38. Precinct: Broad Walk Harlow

testimony to the enlightened attitude of its founder William Lever, (later the first Viscount Leverhulme), who collaborated with a number of designers and architects (notably Lutyens) in its planning.

Port Sunlight was begun in 1888 and by the turn of the century over 480 houses had been built. There are now 1372 houses, though few of them are alike. They all belong to the half timbered style of architecture. There are groups of three and groups of seven. Streets are clearly defined but by subtle variations of alignment and siting monotony has been avoided. The houses have front gardens but, as in old English villages or modern American suburbs there are no enclosing railings or front gates. At the rear of the house are service roads and allotment gardens, but the houses are skilfully grouped so that this necessarily untidy area is rarely seen from the principal roads.

The fierce determination of the founder to respect individuality seems to have avoided the worst consequences that might have flowed

from such excessive patronage of the workers by the employers. But Port Sunlight does represent the first attempt by an industrialist to give his workers an environment with features hitherto confined to the middle classes —lavish greenery and landscaping—and it may have had some influence on the later planning thought of Unwin (q.v.) and Parker (q.v.).

FURTHER READING

Creese, W. J. (1966). *The Search for Environment. (The Garden City Before and After.)*
Bell, Colin and Rose (1969). *City Fathers.*
Pevsner, Nikolaus (1971). *The Buildings of England: Cheshire.*

PRECINCT

This word is often used in conjunction with others like pedestrian and shopping. It means a readily recognisable area the boundary of which is clear and within which certain characteristics exist. So a shopping precinct is one in which shopping is the paramount activity. A pedestrian precinct has the distinct characteristic of providing traffic-free areas in which people may walk in safety.

Nowadays the word usually carries with it the connotation of 'traffic-free' and a place described as a 'shopping' or 'university' or 'office' precinct may be expected to offer a system of purely pedestrian ways and squares with cars parked on the perimeter and vehicle access provided to the rear of the buildings. It is becoming fairly common for existing streets to be closed to traffic and converted into precincts. Examples may be found at Norwich and Bolton.

FURTHER READING

Johnson-Marshall, Percy (1966). *Rebuilding Cities.*

Norwich City Council (1969). *London Street.*

Rudolsky, Bernard (1969). *Streets for People.*

PRESERVATION POLICY GROUP

A Group set up by the Minister of Housing and local Government in 1966 to supervise and consider the results of the Four Town Reports (q.v.), to review progress in the preservation of other historic towns, to consider the preservation measures adopted in other countries and, in the light of these findings, to recommend what changes were desirable in current legal, financial and administrative arrangements for preservation. The report of the Group was published in January 1971.

PURCHASE NOTICE

No one has the right to develop his land, so refusal of planning permission is not a reason in itself for compensation. But if the refusal prevents him from obtaining reasonably beneficial use (q.v.) an owner may serve a Purchase Notice on the local planning authority (q.v.) requiring it to buy the land at a fair price. Refusal of listed building consent (see Listed Building) carries the same provision with it.

Not many purchase notices are served due to the difficulty of proving loss of beneficial use. Loss of some development value is not enough. They have been quite frequently served by owner-occupiers of houses or shops or small businesses, not following refusal of planning consent, but as a result of being unable to sell their premises (as a result of intended development by some public agency) except at a very reduced price. This Planning Blight (q.v.) has thus resulted in many local authorities having to buy such affected property at a fair price.

FURTHER READING

Heap, Desmond (5th Ed. 1970). *An Outline of Planning Law.*

R

RADBURN

A satellite town of New York, New Jersey, which has given its name to a particular type of housing layout, first used there and designed by Clarence Stein (q.v.).

The word is now used very generally to describe a housing layout in which vehicles and pedestrians are segregated by keeping one side of the house (usually the front) free of vehicles, and keeping a 'rear' access road for servicing, garaging, etc.

Originally, the concept was more thorough and precise. At Radburn itself, all fast-moving traffic was restricted to feeder roads from which led culs-de-sac. Houses were grouped around these, one side of the house being accessible from the service roads or courts. On the other side the houses had communal gardens opening onto a pedestrian walkway which led into a central green or park. On the opposite side of the park were more houses grouped around their own service culs-de-sac.

There have been many variations of the idea over the years and the idea has been most extensively used in the New Towns (q.v.).

FURTHER READING

Ministry of Transport (1963). *Traffic in Towns* (Buchanan Report).

Morris, A. E. J. (1970). 'The Radburn Dilemma'; *Official Architecture & Planning*, Vol. 33. May.

Stein, Clarence (1951). *Towards New Towns for America.*

RASMUSSEN, Dr Steen Eiler, 1898–

Danish architect, teacher and populariser, whose lucid books on architecture and planning are widely used in universities and have probably aroused in many people their first conscious awareness and appreciation of their urban surroundings.

In his first book, *London: the Unique City* (1934) Rasmussen postulates two distinct types of city, the scattered and the concentrated or the English and the continental. Taking London as a uniquely developed example of the former, he explores the manner of and reasons for its organic growth and the characteristics that distinguish it from most other capitals. *Towns and Buildings Described in Drawings and Words* (1949) attempts to interest the reader not so much in individual buildings, which Rasmussen considers to be adequately described in guidebooks and elsewhere, but in 'the city as an entity which expresses certain ideals and ways of life', while *Experiencing Architecture* (1957) discusses the architectural elements of texture, scale, proportion, colour, solids and voids and so on and examines the ways in which they have been used by different architects at different times. Each book is written to appeal to the layman and the young as well as to the professional and each derives from Rasmussen's belief that 'it is important to tell people outside our profession what we are engaged on'.

Rasmussen received his professional training at the Architectural School of the Danish Academy (1916–18) and in an architect's office (1918–22) and has been Professor at the Royal Academy of Fine Arts in Copenhagen since 1938.

39. Regional Shopping Centre

He has been President of the Danish Town Planning Institute (1942–8), President of the Copenhagen Regional Town Planning Committee (1945–58). visiting Professor at Massachusetts Institute of Technology (1953), and at Yale University (1954), and Lethaby Professor of Architecture at the Royal College of Art in London (1958). He was appointed Honorary Royal Designer for Industry by the Royal Society of Arts (London) in 1947 and is an Honorary Corresponding Member of the Royal Institute of British Architects (q.v.). In addition to the popular books previously described he has published books and articles in Denmark, Sweden and Germany on industrial art, textiles, architecture and planning.

REGIONAL SHOPPING CENTRE

A specially designed shopping area, usually sited in open country or a suburban area. The idea behind the centre is to provide the widest possible range of shops, with easy access for the private car. Not yet common in Britain but seen frequently in the U.S.A., these centres are often entirely covered over and air conditioned. They are equipped with restaurants, news theatres and crèches as well as department stores and shops. The larger ones may cover as much as 70 acres with another similar acreage devoted to car parking. From the most distant parking lot to the shops may be quite a walk.

Regional shopping centres, as their name implies, serve a wide area. They certainly contributed to the decline of the central areas of some major American cities. It is the fear that there would be a similar impact on existing city centres in the U.K. that has led planning authorities to refuse permission for regional shopping centres.

The term is synonymous with 'out-of-town' shopping centre.

FURTHER READING
Jones, Colin S. (1969). *Regional Shopping Centres: their Location, Planning and Design.*

REHABILITATION

As it implies, the term used to describe the idea of repairing, redecorating and in some cases converting, existing structurally sound property to a standard compatible with modern requirements of amenity and health, for use for a period of 20–30 years. Within the last five years the process has been helped by grants (q.v.), the declaration of Improvement Areas (q.v.) and the whole concept of Environmental Recovery (q.v.).

FURTHER READING
(see Environmental Recovery)

REILLY, Sir Charles Herbert, 1874–1948

Architect, writer, publicist and teacher renowned for his achievements while head of the architectural department of Liverpool University in the first decades of this century.

In 1904 when Reilly was appointed to the Roscoe Chair of Architecture, the school consisted of twelve part-time students doing a two-year course: when he relinquished it in 1933, 200 students were studying a five-year course. But that is a partial and merely numerical measure of an achievement which also consisted of bringing about fundamental changes in both the structure of the department and the quality of its teaching. In 1909, with an endowment from W. H. Lever (who had created Port Sunlight (q.v.)), Reilly established a Chair of Civic Design within the architectural school and thus formed the first university town planning department in Britain. He asked his friend Stanley Adshead (q.v.) to become its first lecturer and to edit its journal, *The Town Planning Review.* As a member of the Educational Board of R.I.B.A. (q.v.), he championed the cause of university training (rather than office apprenticeship) for architects and was eventually able to institute degree courses, while by his frequent visits to the U.S.A., and as corresponding member of the American Institute of Planners (from 1925), he established an understanding and sympathy with the American architectural and planning profession that was to influence a whole generation of his students. Liverpool became 'the first of the great architectural schools to which the new race of office-liberated students flocked'* and emerged as an influential and

* Stanley C. Ramsay, 'Charles Herbert Reilly'. *The Book of Liverpool School of Architecture.* Ed. Lionel Budden. Liverpool University Press 1932, pp. 26–7.

84

widely respected centre of architectural and planning studies.

Reilly's other activities were as many as they were varied. Throughout his career he was an accomplished journalist whose reviews and articles in magazines and newspapers, amongst them the *Architectural Review*, the *Builders Journal*, the *Liverpool Post* and the *Manchester Guardian*, appealed as much to the layman as to the professional. In early years while in private practice he designed a number of buildings in London including an unusually attractive Generating Station in Marylebone (1904) and St Barnabas Church, Hackney (1910) and later, as consultant, he influenced the siting of the Liverpool entrance into the Mersey Tunnel, and the designs of Devonshire House (1923) in Piccadilly and the Peter Jones department store (1936) in Sloane Square—London's first curtain-walled building. He visited New Delhi (q.v.) with Lutyens and was architectural editor of *Country Life* (1922). His idea for placing houses informally around small greens was adopted at Bilston and Dudley, and became an accepted planning concept known as the Reilly Green. Each of these activities contributed not only to his own reputation but also to the standing of Liverpool University.

Reilly was Vice-President of the R.I.B.A. (1931–3) and was awarded its Gold Medal in 1943. He was knighted in 1944.

His published works are:

Some Liverpool Streets and Buildings (1921).
Some Architectural Problems of Today (1924).
McKim, Mead and White (1924).
Some Manchester Streets and Buildings (1924).
Representative of British Architecture in the Present Day (1931).
The Theory and Practice of Architecture (1932).
Scaffolding in the Sky (Autobiography) (1938).
Outline Plan for Birkenhead (1947).

RE-LOCATION

A continuous by-product of planning and renewal is the enforced displacement of 'non-conforming uses'—usually commercial undertakings of one sort or another. The reason for disturbance may also be the construction of new roads.

In either case (whilst the local planning authority (q.v.), having paid appropriate compensation, has no legal obligation to do so) if disruption of business is to be avoided, or minimised, it is a wise provision of planning to have a policy of re-locating disturbed businesses in appropriately located reception areas.

Any local planning authority which has a genuine policy of re-location, will follow one or more of the following courses of action:

(a) It will have a 'bank' of suitable older property, unlikely to be re-developed for some years, which can be offered to disturbed users at relatively low rents because of its age.

(b) It will acquire sites which can be offered on building leases to those who themselves are able to build.

(c) It will acquire land and erect buildings for offer on lease at reasonable rents for those unable to build themselves.

The problem of re-location of commercial enterprises is a very vexed one. Often businesses are in existence only because of extremely low rentals and over-heads. Any disturbance means they cease to operate. There is always dispute about the level of rents on re-location. And an inability to meet new rents may mean the business is not genuinely viable anyway. But rents asked are sometimes excessive.

Much abortive work may be done by local planning authorities. A business owner may negotiate for many months for a new site or building and then, at the last, decide to simply accept compensation and go out of business.

Re-location of residents when their homes are disturbed is of course different, in that the local authority is legally obliged to offer alternative accommodation.

FURTHER READING
Cullingworth, J. B. (3rd Ed. 1969). *Town and Country Planning in England and Wales.*
Keeble, Lewis (4th Ed. 1970). *Principles and Practice of Town and Country Planning.*

R.F.A.C. (*see* Royal Fine Art Commission).

opposite
Rehabilitation
40 & 41. The Giles, Pitterweem, Fife, before and after

85

Princes Jetty

Princes Landing Stage

Princes Stage

Liverpool Landing Stage

(Floating)

Floating Bridge

Ferry

Queensway

(Mersey Tunnel)

Lime Street Station

DOCKS

Kent Gardens

Goods Sta

High Water Mark of Medium Tides

Mud and Sand

Low Water Mark of Medium Tides

0   1/4   1/2 mile.

R.I.B.A. (*see* Royal Institute of British Architects).

RIBBON DEVELOPMENT

The practice, very common between the two World Wars and still noticeable today, of building (particularly houses) along either side of main roads. This development was often only one building plot deep, with open country behind. The result contributed largely to the blurring of the edges of town and country, and encouraged the impression of one town connecting directly with its neighbour. It was an extremely wasteful method of developing in that it frequently made large tracts of backland incapable of development.

FURTHER READING
Cullen, Gordon (1961). *Townscape.*

RING ROAD

A term applied to any road which encircles the centre of a town. Ring roads are generally defined as 'inner', 'intermediate' or 'outer'. Nowadays the term may be used to describe a motorway standard road, but in its original form it was usually dual-carriageway, fairly rigidly geometrical and having roads radiating through it from the town centre. Its function was, and still often is even in its modern counterparts, to enable traffic travelling towards a town to gain access to a location on the opposite side without passing through the town centre, or to speed up traffic journeying from one side of town to another.

FURTHER READING
British Road Federation (1956). *Urban Motorways.*
Davies, Ernest (Ed.) (1960). *Roads and Their Traffic.*

ROEHAMPTON

One of the finest and largest low cost local authority housing schemes in the world. Situated near Richmond Park, London, in wooded and undulating parkland, formerly the grounds of some Victorian houses. The mixed development consists of ten- and eleven-storey 'point' blocks, six-storey slab blocks, four-storey maisonette blocks, two- and three-storey terrace houses and one storey, one room, dwellings for old people. The highest buildings are on the highest ground with the 'point' blocks grouped at east and west and balanced in the total composition by the large slab blocks placed on a gentle slope towards the centre of

42. Ring Road: Liverpool
43. Roehampton

the site. These are surfaced in rough concrete and raised on stilts in a manner explicitly reminiscent of Le Corbusier's (q.v.) Unités d'Habitation at Marseilles and Nantes.

The diversity of building types, the curving roads and the care with which every tree and natural feature has been consciously used in the design, create an environment of ever-changing views and contrasts, while in the slab region, where the design is visually the most impressive, the combination of tough architectural mass and continuous parkland recalls the achievements of eighteenth-century spas and resorts.

Immediately renowned for its visual qualities, imaginative land use and advanced construction techniques, the Roehampton estate has more recently been criticized for its lack of community facilities, local shops and neighbourhood atmosphere.

It was built between 1952–6, covers 128 acres and accommodates 9,500 people in 2,611 dwellings at a density of 110 people to the built-up acre. The architects were the London County Council team under Sir Leslie Martin.

FURTHER READING
Kidder Smith, G. E. (1962). *The New Architecture of Europe*.

ROTTERDAM

The Lijnbaan shopping area in Rotterdam, part of the reconstruction of the city centre following its almost total obliteration in the blitz of 1940, is widely held to be one of the most successful and attractive post-war shopping developments in Europe or America.

The decision to plan comprehensively and boldly was taken early at Rotterdam as it had been at Coventry (q.v.): an outline plan had been prepared within four weeks of the bombing. By compulsorily acquiring about two thirds of the blitzed area the Government also ensured that the municipal authority would have firm control over the planning of the new development. In view of this, and with the benefit of hindsight, it is perhaps easy to be disappointed in what appear to be missed opportunities in the plan. Its framework con-

sists of three major north–south roads intersecting three major east–west roads at roundabouts. One of them is the Coolsingel Boulevard, the traditional centre of the shopping area, widened to 200 feet. As a result the Town Hall, Post Office and Stock Exchange on its east side, among the very few buildings to survive the blitz and therefore natural focal points in the city, are separated from the main commercial area to the west by a wide road of both parked and swiftly moving vehicles.

While some may like the spaciousness and activity of this and other main shopping streets, planners have been almost universally impressed by the traffic-free Lijnbaan shopping area. This is cruciform in shape and consists of two-storey shops aligned along comparatively narrow and intimate pedestrian malls of 39 and 59 foot width. Continuous canopies provide shelter and maintain the intimate scale while cross canopies help to break the linear space into smaller compartments. The showcases, pieces of sculpture, benches, exotic flowers and outdoor café all contribute to the feel of a place designed for meeting as well as shopping, while the eight- and fourteen-storey blocks of flats placed behind the shops provide big city scale and excitement, contrast effectively with the low shops and represent a conscious attempt to prevent the city life dying with the evening.

The scheme was in fact a modification of the earlier plan and the result of close co-operation between the planning department, the architects, Van Den Broek and Bakema, and the shopkeepers' association which now has responsibility for looking after the advertisements and street furniture (q.v.).

It is of course, possible to criticise aspects of the Lijnbaan development. Although one of the pedestrian ways is terminated visually by the Town Hall, the whole development, and indeed the whole central area, has been thought to lack any one focal point. The layout of the blocks of flats might be considered too regimented. Car parking provision is inadequate. If

opposite
Rotterdam
44 & 45. Two views of the Lijnbaan traffic-free shopping centre

the development were planned today, it is likely that the roofs of the shopping units would be used as circulation or recreation space associated with the flats.

The development is nevertheless an imaginative and outstanding achievement of its time and, like the precincts at Coventry (q.v.), has helped to persuade shopkeepers and planners alike of the benefits and sanity of creating pedestrian shopping areas both in redevelopment schemes and in existing town and city centres.

FURTHER READING

Johnson-Marshall, Percy (1966). *Rebuilding Cities.*

Gibberd, Frederick (1959). *Town Design.*

Mumford, L. (1961). *The City in History.*

Bacon, E. N. (1967). *Design of Cities.*

ROUNDABOUT

A single level junction between two or more roads, designed to allow movement from one road to another without stopping by using the principle of weaving (q.v.). The circumference of the central circular reservation has to be sufficient to provide enough road length between the various roads to permit vehicles to change lanes (q.v.) and cross each others' paths.

ROYAL FINE ART COMMISSION

The Royal Fine Art Commission was set up in 1924 and consists of seventeen members appointed by Royal Warrant. Its function is to offer expert advice in a most difficult area of planning—that of aesthetic design. Anyone may consult the R.F.C.A. but it has to give its advice to a public or quasi public body. It is consulted by a large number of people with very different interests and is empowered to report on its own initiative on matters it considers important.

Many of its achievements are by persuasion, but it does issue fairly outspoken reports and comments on such subjects as power stations, new buildings in historic areas (e.g. office blocks close to a medieval cathedral). Its

opinions are not always accepted and are not thought by some members of the architectural profession to be unchallengeably correct! It would be surprising if its recommendations met with ready acceptance all the time but it does perform a useful role in a difficult area and gets through a large amount of work. It often feels that, even when its basic recommendations have been rejected, it should continue to try to secure such detailed improvements as it can. Unfortunately this leads the general public to regard it as partially responsible for the final appearance of a building with which it may have no sympathy at all.

FURTHER READING

Royal Fine Art Commission. *Annual Reports.*

ROYAL INSTITUTE OF BRITISH ARCHITECTS

The Royal Institute of British Architects exists to promote the highest standards in architecture, and to conserve or improve the architectural environment. Founded in 1834, the Institute received its first Royal Charter in 1837. Its purposes were expressed in that Charter as being for 'the general advancement of civil architecture and for promoting and facilitating the acquirement of the knowledge of the various Arts and Sciences connected therewith'.

The R.I.B.A. is both a professional institute and a learned society. Its membership is some 20,000 (excluding students) in the United Kingdom and 5,000 overseas. 50 per cent in private practice, 40 per cent in public service of one sort or another and the rest in teaching or industry. Most practising architects in the U.K. are members.

In its role as a professional institute the R.I.B.A. has from the outset established the integrity and responsibility of its members by its code of professional conduct. Since 1882 its examinations have been compulsory and since 1931 no one may call himself an 'architect' until he has passed the examinations of the Institute (or those recognised as equivalent by the Institute). Having once passed he becomes registered with the Architects' Registration Council of the U.K., which allows him to practise and he need not then become a member of the Institute although most do.

As a learned society the R.I.B.A. raises the level of knowledge and the standard of practice, by publishing a journal and a range of aids to practising architects and by arranging lectures, meetings, symposia and conferences. Its library is the finest national collection of architectural books and drawings.

ADDRESS
RIBA, 66, Portland Place, London, W1N 4AD.

FURTHER READING
Royal Institute of British Architects (Bi Annual) *Directory.*

ROYAL TOWN PLANNING INSTITUTE
Formally founded in 1914, the R.T.P.I. is the professional institute of planners in the U.K. With 6,755 members and students it is one of the smaller institutes but is growing very rapidly, having grown from 64 members at the start. It was granted permission to use the prefix 'Royal' in 1971.

Leading figures in the formation of the Institute were Thomas Adams, J. W. Cockrill, Raymond Unwin, Patrick Geddes and George Pepler. It has as its stated purpose in its Royal Charter (obtained in 1959):

(a) The advancement of the study of Town Planning and of the arts and sciences applied thereto.

(b) The promotion of the artistic and scientific development of towns, cities and the countryside.

(c) The securing of the association of those engaged or interested professionally or otherwise in Town Planning and the promotion of their general interests.

Fellows (F.R.T.P.I.), Members (M.R.T.P.I.), Legal Members (L.M.R.T.P.I.), and Legal Associate Members (L.A.M.R.T.P.I.) are entitled to use the designation 'Chartered Town Planner' which is the recognised technical qualification for town and country planning appointments in the public service and in private practice in the United Kingdom and in many overseas countries.

The R.T.P.I. Journal is published ten times a year, but views expressed in it are not necessarily the views of the Institute.

ADDRESS
Royal Town Planning Inst., 26, Portland Place, London, W1.

FURTHER READING
R.T.P.I. Yearbook (Annual).

R.T.P.I. (see Royal Town Planning Institute).

S

SALTAIRE
The most widely acclaimed of several mid-nineteenth-century model towns and villages built by philanthropic industrialists in an endeavour to provide healthier living conditions for their work-people than could be obtained in the major industrial cities.

Saltaire (1853–71) was built by Sir Titus Salt four miles north of Bradford, close to the river Aire and provided dwellings for a substantial proportion of the 3,000 employees at his newly built alpaca wool factory. 850 terrace

houses were aligned along a regular grid of streets at a density of 32 to the acre. Few had front gardens. Although the town was thus not immediately distinguishable from a typical urban working class housing area, almshouses, a complete drainage system, allotments and a public park represented a considerable advance in community planning. The large number of three-bedroomed houses and the survey of workers' needs on which the house designs were based, were also notable features at this time. An Institution where culture, but not

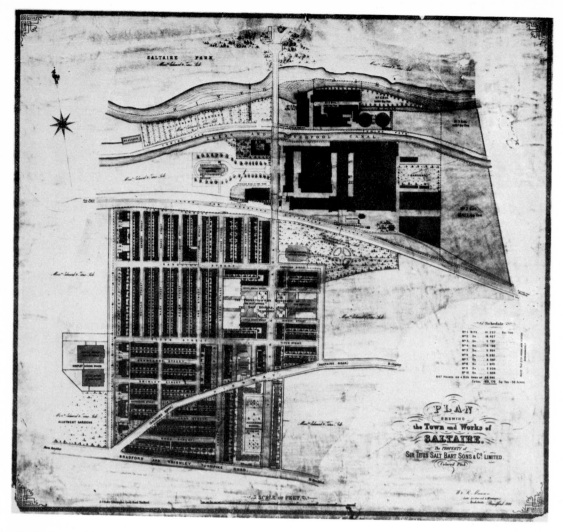

46. Saltaire: Plan

alcohol, could be acquired and an unstinted supply of chapels and places of worship indicated that Salt's non-conformist and paternalistic zeal was not confined to improving the physical health of his workers.

Saltaire is no longer a self-sufficient community and speculative development has encroached on its rural surroundings. It nevertheless retains a distinct visual identity.

The gridiron layout has been both criticised for its unimaginative disregard of the contours of the site and admired for its compactness; it was this last quality that particularly appealed to those who, in the 1950s, found the open and low density (q.v.) layouts of the Mark I New Towns (q.v.) wanting in urbanity.

Other model villages of this period were Bessbrook in Ireland (1846), Copley (1849), Akroydon (1869), West Hill Park near Halifax and Bromborough Pool in the Wirrall. Although they were models that went uncopied they were notable landmarks in that search for a better environment through re-settlement which links the writings and projects of Robert Owen and James Silk Buckingham to the creation of the British post-war New Towns (q.v.).

FURTHER READING
Creese, W. J. (1966). *The Search for Environment (The Garden City Before and After)*.
Bell, Colin and Rose (1969). *City Fathers*.

Ashworth, W. (1954). *The Genesis of Modern British Town Planning*.

Balgarnie (1878). *Sir Titus Salt: His Life and its Lessons*.

Cherry, G. E. (1970). *Town Planning in its Social Context*.

SANDYS, Duncan, 1908–

Has a particular place in British Town Planning principally for his role as founder of the Civic Trust (q.v.) in 1957. Prior to that he was, from 1954–7, Minister of Housing and Local Government and it was during this period that he came to recognise the need for an independent organisation capable of commenting on bad design and planning and campaigning for better standards.

Amongst his major achievements in a long and distinguished public life, covering most aspects of Government, should be listed his Civic Amenities Act (q.v.) which he steered through Parliament with the support of both parties.

In 1970 he became President of Europa Nostra, a European organisation concerned about the preservation of Europe's Architectural and Historical Heritage.

SANT' ELIA, Antonio, 1880–1916

A brilliant young Italian architect and theorist whose visionary project *La Città Nuova*, exhibited at Milan in 1914, was one of the first and most influential of a number of intensely lyrical evocations of the technological city of the future published in the first decades of this century.

The exhibition showed impressionistic sketches of a multi-level imaginary city of towering skyscrapers with external liftshafts, motorways, bridges and viaducts, vast factories and a complex multi-storey interchange building for road, railway and air transport. It was a declaration of faith in the big city or metropolitan idea, and was accompanied by an impassioned *Messaggio* pleading for a 'new state of mind' and a new architecture to embrace and exploit the potentialities of the industrialised machine age. 'We must invent and build *ex novo* our Modern City like an immense and tumultuous shipyard, active, mobile and everywhere dynamic and the modern building like a gigantic machine. . . . The house of concrete, iron and glass, without painting or sculpture . . . brutish in its mechanical simplicity must rise from the brink of a tumultuous abyss, the street . . . gathering up the traffic of the metropolis connected for necessary transfers to metal cat-walks and high-speed conveyor belts.'

Although Sant' Elia was killed in action in the First World War at the age of 36 before any of his designs had been built, the ideas contained in his *Messaggio* had been propagated throughout Europe by publication (with a few modifications) as the centre piece of the Futurist Manifesto of Modern Architecture (1914). This Manifesto, with its glorification of speed, movement and plasticity is considered to have influenced both the expressionist movement in architecture and Le Corbusier (q.v.) (in particular his concept of a City for Three Million People).

One of Sant' Elia's designs for a house has been executed posthumously in Como where a permanent exhibition of his works has also been opened.

FURTHER READING

Apollonia, Umbro (1958). *Antonio Sant' Elia*, Milan.

Sartoris, Alberto (1930). *Antonio Sant' Elia*, Milan.

Pevsner, Nikolaus (1968). *The Sources of Modern Architecture and Design*.

Pevsner, Nikolaus (1970). *Pioneers of Modern Design*.

SATELLITE TOWN

This term was often used in the years immediately after the First World War as an alternative to 'Garden City'. It stressed the importance of garden cities as distinct self-contained 'civic units' dependent for their life on great cities. It also has a much wider meaning that includes any town that is closely related to a larger city yet is physically separate from it and has a corporate life of its own. It had a specific meaning for R. G. R. Taylor in his book *Satellite*

Cities (1915) as a description of industrial suburbs built around the edges of large American cities.

The term 'satellite' was adopted from astronomical science to mean a body that is within the influence of another more powerful body, revolving around it, yet physically distinct. Howard's (q.v.) diagram showing satellite garden cities has a distinct astronomical flavour.

FURTHER READING

Howard, Ebenezer (later edition 1946). *Garden Cities of Tomorrow.*

Osborn, F. J. and Whittick, A. (2nd Ed. 1969). *New Towns: the Answer to Megalopolis.*

Purdom, C. B. (2nd Ed. 1949). *The Building of Satellite Towns.*

SATURATION LEVEL

The state of affairs in any area when the ratio of cars to population ceases to show a material annual increase. Another use of the phrase is now becoming common; a road may be said to be approaching saturation level when no increase in the number of vehicles is possible without traffic movement being totally stopped.

FURTHER READING

Davies, Ernest (Ed.) (1960). *Roads and Their Traffic.*

Ministry of Transport (1963). *Traffic in Towns.* (Buchanan Report).

SCOTT COMMITTEE

On Land Utilisation in Rural Areas. The Committee was set up in 1941 (along with the Beveridge Committee on Social Insurance and Allied Services and the Uthwatt Committee (q.v.) on Compensation and Betterment) to consider one aspect of the problems of postwar reconstruction.

The committee's terms of reference were 'to consider the conditions which should govern building and other constructional development in country areas consistent with the maintenance of agriculture, and in particular the factors affecting the location of industry, having regard to economic operation, part

time and seasonal employment, the well-being of rural communities and the preservation of rural amenities'. The committee's belief that they should interpret their terms widely, including the sense that rural amenities meant a national heritage, led them to recommend such ideas as National Parks (q.v.) and nature reserves.

FURTHER READING

Cullingworth, J. B. (3rd Ed. 1970). *Town and Country Planning in England and Wales.*

SEMI-MATURE TREE PLANTING

In the 1950s following the speed of building that had resulted from new techniques, the need for large trees in association with new buildings became widely felt. Until then the moving of semi-mature trees had only been possible at considerable cost and in a laborious manner.

In 1958 the Civic Trust (q.v.) began to explore the possibilities of moving large numbers of trees (up to 25' high) and developed a new technique and trailer for the work. Between 1961 and 1963 the Trust itself moved over 650 trees and claims an 80 per cent success. The technique, now commercially employed by many firms, depends for success on careful selection of types, root pruning of trees some 12–18 months in advance, proper preparation of the hole to receive the root-ball, great care of the root-ball during movement and subsequent care of the tree once moved. If any one of these aspects is neglected then failure may follow.

Following the pioneer work of the Trust, the National Coal Board Opencast Executive began to develop the idea and now moves thousands of trees a month, using a different type of mechanical scoop which lifts, transports and re-plants the tree in one operation. Root pruning is not done in this case.

The idea of transplanting semi-mature trees trees has been heavily criticised and debate continues about the best techniques. But there

opposite
Semi-Mature Tree Planting
47 & 48. Jarrow, Co. Durham, before and after

94

seems little doubt that, if properly done, it can succeed and certainly the impact of a group of semi-mature trees in a new development cannot be achieved any other way.

FURTHER READING
Civic Trust (1967). *The Civic Trust Trees Campaign.*

SERVICE INDUSTRY

Basic or manufacturing industries are fairly obvious but there are a great many other activities, not readily housed in offices or shops, which are a vital part of, and provide an important service to, the community. It is these that are, somewhat misleadingly, classified as service industries. The log merchant, rag and bone merchant, laundry, service garage, builder's yard, local authority depot are typical of this classification.

Their siting to a large extent is related to their function, some having to be central to the area they serve. Argument has taken place about their being segregated from other uses. Clearly some are noisy or unsightly and need to be accommodated on specially located and prepared sites. Others can happily be incorporated into residential or commercial areas.

One common feature of most such industries is their lack of working capital and provision has to be made in any plan for a site where they can function harmlessly and can be allowed to erect the most makeshift of buildings. In recent years many local authorities have provided such sites and others have gone as far as erecting simple structures for such industries to rent—often at a subsidised figure initially.

SHANKLAND, Colin Graeme Lindsay, 1917–

Graeme Shankland is one of the distinguished British town planners to emerge after the Second World War. Initially concerned with British projects, his work (now in partnership with Oliver Cox) has developed into a world-wide practice.

After training at Cambridge University and the Architectural Association, Shankland began his professional career with the London County Council and was closely involved in the re-development of the South Bank and the Elephant and Castle. Towards the end of the fifties he began to emerge as an original thinker and produced an innovative study for a new suburb of London called *The Living Suburb—Boston Manor Study.* When the London County Council embarked on its imaginative new town concept at Hook (q.v.), Shankland was Senior Architect Planner and on its abandonment was responsible for the report's publication.

In 1962 Shankland started in private practice when appointed planning consultant to Liverpool Corporation (q.v.). Involving the re-development of the city centre and its major highway network, the consultancy broke new ground in presenting its advice in a series of interval reports rather than one masterplan at the end of the study.

In the years that followed, Shankland's office was given commissions for Bolton town centre, the expansion of Ipswich, the redevelopment at Kingston, Jamaica. This saw the beginning of the international practice and was followed by work in France (Pontoise) and the United States of America (a plan for a residential community at Staten Island). Work in Yugoslavia, Iran, Brazil, Egypt, Peru, and Malaysia was commissioned by the United Nations. At home, Shankland was involved with Llewellyn Davies, Weeks, Forestier-Walker and Bor on the planning implications of developing the four short-listed sites for the Third London Airport, at the request of the Roskill Commission.

SHARP, Thomas Wilfrid, 1910–

Author, planning consultant and authority on village designs, Thomas Sharp spent his childhood in Durham mining villages and received no formal professional training in planning. After early years spent in local government he became Senior Research Officer of the Ministry of Town and Country Planning (1941–3) where, among other works, he was Secretary of the Scott Committee (q.v.) and Chairman of the Study Group on Site Planning and Layout in Relation to Housing. Later he became lecturer and then Reader in town planning at King's College, Newcastle-upon-Tyne (University of Durham) where he was responsible for establishing the first degree

49. Thomas Sharp

tinue throughout the forties and fifties as the first New Towns (q.v.) were built and which is still finding expression today in, for instance, the special issue of the Architectural Review, *Civilia* (June 1971). *Town and Countryside* was also the first book to stress that the countryside is man-made, not God-given, and therefore requires deliberate and careful maintenance. Sharp developed and popularised these ideas further in *Town Planning* (1940), which at 200,000 copies probably reached a wider audience than any other book on planning, and in his studies, *Exeter Phoenix* (1946) and *Oxford Replanned* (1948), which were the first books published in England to propound the concept of Townscape (q.v.).

One of Sharp's best known works is his *Anatomy of the Village* (1946) which was the first attempt to examine the physical and social characteristics of the English village in planning terms and to suggest how they might be created and maintained in the future. Sharp has since designed four new villages in Northumberland for the Forestry Commission (q.v.) and a new seaside village at Port Eynon in South Wales.

Sharp has been President of the Royal Town Planning Institute (q.v.) (1945–6) and of the Institute of Landscape Architects (q.v.) (1949–1951). He is a Fellow of the Royal Institute of British Architects (q.v.) and was awarded the C.B.E. in 1951. His books not previously mentioned are:

The Future Development of South-West Lancashire (1930).
A Derelict Area (1935).
English Panorama (1937).
Cathedral City (1945).
A Plan for Taunton (1948).
Georgian City; Chichester (1949).
Newer Sarum (1949).
Oxford Observed (1952).
Design in Town and Country (part) (1953).
Dreaming Spires and Teeming Towers, the character of Cambridge (1963).
Town and Townscape (1968).

course in town planning in Britain and the Commonwealth.

During these years and since, Sharp has been consultant in private practice responsible for development plans (q.v.) for a number of places including Durham, Exeter, Oxford, Salisbury, Chichester, Todmorden, St Andrew's, Taunton, King's Lynn, Stockport, Minehead, Kensington and Rugby. Each plan is notable for its thorough, detailed and sensitive appreciation of those qualities that give to each town its individual character.

This feeling for the particular identity of a place consistently informs Sharp's many writings and has kindled in many people, planners and laymen alike, their first appreciation of the qualities of the English town and countryside.

His first book, *Town and Countryside* (1932) was the first sustained critique of the Garden City idea as manifest in Letchworth (q.v.) and Welwyn (q.v.), and a plea for a more urban and compact manner of building. It marked the beginning of a divergence of opinion about architectural and town design that was to con-

SILKIN, Lewis (Lord) 1889–1972

Silkin earned an indelible place in the history of planning by the legislation which he introduced into Parliament while Minister of Town and Country Planning from 1945–50.

Both the New Towns Act 1946 (q.v.) and the Town and Country Planning Act 1947 were of outstanding importance in determining the future quality and direction of planning in Britain and their content and successful passage were in large part due to Silkin's foresight, tenacity and political acumen.

It was perhaps likely that any incoming Government in 1945 would have created at least one or two new towns. Pressure for national policies based on the main recommendations of the Barlow report (q.v.) was mounting. But Silkin's Act was neither an expedient nor a sop. His proposal for 20 new towns and the content of the Act itself ('an essay in civilisation . . . an opportunity to evolve . . . for coming generations the means of a happy and gracious way of life'), represented a wholehearted acceptance of the new town concept. He has justly become known as the father of Britain's New Town programme.

The Town and Country Planning Act 1947 was no less innovatory, transferring planning powers from district to county councils (q.v.), and making the preparation of Development Plans (q.v.) a statutory responsibility throughout the country. Plans prepared by local authorities were for the first time capable of adaptation to meet new circumstances without reference to Parliament, the concept of Listed Buildings (q.v.) was introduced, and planning became generally more comprehensive and less regulatory. Despite the eventual failure of its financial provisions, the 1947 Act provided the framework for all subsequent planning legislation and the model upon which statutory planning has since been based in many parts of the world.

Silkin's last notable achievement as Minister was the National Parks and Access to the Countryside Act 1949, which introduced National Parks (q.v.) and Areas of Outstanding Natural Beauty (q.v.) as means of ensuring the preservation of our finest countryside.

Before becoming Minister he had been Chairman of the London County Council's Town Planning Committee (1940–5), which had commissioned Sir Patrick Abercrombie's (q.v.) Greater London Plan. Lord Silkin was an honorary Vice-President of the Royal Town Planning Institute (q.v.) and was awarded its Gold Medal in 1971.

FURTHER READING

Ashworth, W. (1954). *The Genesis of Modern British Town Planning.*

Osborn F. J. and Whittick, Arnold (2nd Ed. 1969). *The New Towns: the Answer to Megalopolis.*

SITTE, Camillo, 1843–1903

Austrian art historian and writer whose book *Der Städtebau nach seinen künstlerischen Grundsätzen* (City Planning According to Artistic Principles), published in 1889, had a profound influence on the planning profession and established a method of analysing the structure of towns and cities that is still widely advocated and employed today.

Der Städtebau had its origins in Sitte's distaste for the regular and classical mode of town planning as exemplified, in particular, in the contemporary Ringstrasse development around Vienna which was probably inspired by Haussmann (q.v.). In order to illuminate what he considered to be its failings, he made an extended analysis, with sketches and plans, of the visual characteristics of several historical pre-industrial cities which had developed organically and casually over a span of centuries. In each case, underlying an apparently haphazard layout, he was able to identify three main organising principles of irregularity, asymmetry and enclosure. Buildings had been related to each other to create a sequence of interrelated, enclosed streets and squares in which space was clearly defined. Breaks in the building line, differences of level and the asymmetrical placing of monuments, trees and statues had been used to create unexpected and constantly changing views. Buildings had been carefully related in height and scale to the size of the spaces they surrounded. In Sitte's view, these principles had created cities that, in their compactness and informality, provided more protection from inclement weather and were visually and psychologically more satisfying than contemporary redevelopment and town extension schemes with their regular layouts, formal symmetrical squares, isolated buildings, relentlessly straight streets and emphasis on traffic engineering. He recognised that the principles had evolved from an 'innate, instinctive aesthetic sense' which had since been lost, but offered his book and the systematic method of visual analysis it demonstrated as a means whereby his contemporaries could consciously recapture it.

Sitte's ideas were enthusiastically received and within a month of publication *Der Städtebau* had entered its second edition. Sitte himself, Director of the State School of Industrial Arts in Vienna and sometime architect, artist, scenographer, teacher and journalist, was invited to become consultant to several municipal authorities. His book was eventually translated into at least five foreign languages and, both during his life and posthumously, its ideas became the centre of controversial disputes within the planning profession. Perhaps his influence abroad was greatest in England where it was acknowledged by Patrick Geddes (q.v.) and Raymond Unwin (q.v.), manifest in the designs for Hampstead Garden Suburb (q.v.) and can be discerned in the writings of Thomas Sharp (q.v.), Frederick Gibberd (q.v.), Gordon Cullen (see Townscape), and, consistently, in the *Architectural Review*.

FURTHER READING
Collins, G. and C. *Camillo Sitte and the Birth of Modern City Planning.*
Chaoy, Françoise (1969). *The Modern City: Planning in the Nineteenth Century.*

SKYLINE

A subject of immense interest to architects and no small significance nationally. The protection of natural skylines from indiscriminate building (which so often destroys scale) and the creation of interesting urban skylines is still a real challenge to designers. In postwar years carelessness about the siting of new tall buildings has often led to the loss of very fine traditional views (e.g. London).

Related to this has been the 'reduction' in size of such large open areas as the London Royal Parks, by the erection of very tall buildings on their periphery.

FURTHER READING
Liverpool City Council (1965). *High Buildings Policy.*
Sharp, Thomas (1968). *Town and Townscape.*

SLIP ROAD

The approach or departure road leading to or from a motorway (q.v.). It is of sufficient length to allow vehicles using it to build up or decrease speed sufficiently to match the speed of vehicles on the road they are joining, without causing obstruction.

FURTHER READING
Drake, James (1969). *Motorways.*

SLUM AND SLUM CLEARANCE

SLUM. Houses in a slum clearance area must be 'dangerous or injurious to the health of the inhabitants of the area by reason of their bad arrangement, or the narrowness or bad arrangement of the streets'.

SLUM CLEARANCE. Since the mid 1950s about two million people have been rehoused as a result of slum clearance programmes. By about 1980 the great majority of housing authorities in Great Britain will have succeeded in getting rid of all their present slums, but clearance will take much longer in some of the bigger local authorities such as Birmingham, Manchester and Liverpool.

Housing authorities are obliged to see that other accommodation exists, or can be provided by them, for people displaced from slum clearance areas. Where an unfit house is demolished by order of the local authority and the owner retains his land, he normally receives no compensation. If the local authority acquire an unfit property in order to demolish it themselves and to rebuild on the land, the normal basis of compensation is the market value of the house as it stands. In England, Wales and Scotland the slum clearance code provides for payments for condemned houses which have

50. Slum

been well maintained although inherently unfit and business occupiers may receive hardship payments in certain cases.

FURTHER READING

Ministry of Housing and Local Government (1966). *The Deeplish Study.*

Jones, Emrys (1966). *Towns and Cities.*

Storm, Michael (1965). *Urban Growth in Britain.*

SOCIETY FOR THE PROMOTION OF URBAN RENEWAL (S.P.U.R.)

Now no longer in existence but historically significant in the work done to focus attention on Urban Renewal (q.v.) in the U.K. after the Second World War. Also interesting as the society in which subsequently eminent people first began to become prominent.

SOCIETY FOR THE PROTECTION OF ANCIENT BUILDINGS (S.P.A.B.)

Was founded on 22 March 1877, as a result of a letter from William Morris to the Athenaeum. It was founded to prevent Victorian 'restoration' and subsequent ruination of churches, too many of which had already been lost. In its original manifesto it was charged with the task of discovering 'how best to protect buildings . . . and otherwise to resist all tampering with either the fabric or the ornament of the building as it stands'. Those principles still guide the society today.

51. Slum Clearance

Whilst its main work is to place its accumulated experience and technical knowledge at the disposal of those who need it the society does work in a number of other ways:

(i) The investigation of cases of buildings suffering from neglect, or threatened with damaging treatment or destruction.

(ii) The preparation of surveys and reports on cities, towns and villages, streets and individual buildings.

(iii) The keeping of records of past repair work and case histories, which are available for study.

(iv) The holding of annual courses on the repair of old buildings.

(v) The administration of the Lethaby and Bannister-Fletcher Scholarships which enables architectural students to study old buildings, their treatment and repair.

From about 1950 the society has produced lists of houses threatened with demolition which are made available to those looking for houses to repair and inhabit.

Though formed originally to care for individual buildings, the society has concerned itself since the middle 1920s with whole towns and groups of buildings.

ADDRESS
Society for the Protection of Ancient Buildings, 55, Great Ormond St, London, WC1.

FURTHER READING
Ward, Pamela (1968). *Conservation and Development.*

STATUTORY UNDERTAKERS
Those bodies, usually nationalised industries, who, by statute, have a duty to provide a certain service for the public at large.

The list of Statutory Undertakers includes The Central Electricity Generating Board, the Regional Electricity Boards, the Gas Council and the Regional Boards, the Forestry Commission, the National Coal Board, British Rail, British Road Services and British Waterways.

In common with Government Departments, statutory undertakers do not come within the control of local Planning Authorities. A process of consultation exists at Central Government level and Local Authorities are kept 'informed'.

The immunity of such bodies to the planning process has been a source of debate and discontent ever since the 1947 Town and Country Planning Act. Many areas of countryside and much urban quality have been spoiled by, for example, the insensitive siting of electricity supply lines, opencast coal mining and the planting of unsuitable trees in 'geometric' plantations. Recently most statutory undertakers have shown greater concern for the environment and now employ skilled designers and landscape architects to help mitigate the impact of their activities.

FURTHER READING
Cullingworth, J. B. (3rd Ed. 1970). *Town and Country Planning in England and Wales.*

STEIN, Clarence 1882–
American architect and planner whose name is inextricably linked with the concept of the Radburn (q.v.) layout and the Greenbelt cities of the American New Deal in the thirties.

In partnership for a decade with Henry Wright, Stein made a mammoth contribution to the planning thought through the American Regional Plan Association and the work he was able to do at Radburn (N.J.), Chatham Village (Pittsburgh), Sunnyside, Baldwin Hills (L.A.) and Greenbelt (Maryland). He was a combination of artist and organiser. With a will of iron, disguised behind a manner of conciliation, he kept the office running and deployed his staff with such skill they acquired an almost unchallenged authority amongst their opponents. He assessed ideas and individuals with great skill, and often his persistence prevented Wright from digressing along interesting intellectual but socially less profitable avenues. This persistence enabled him to nurse Wright through a period of disillusionment with the plan for New York State and allow the birth of a brilliant new concept of decentralisation (q.v.).

Stein's work was carried out against a backcloth of wide public concern for the creation of real communities and his principal and abiding aim was to co-ordinate and mobilise the financial power of the state for the greatest benefit to the whole of society. His statesmanlike approach to urban problems and their solution caused him to become much more than an architect and planner (q.v.). His book *Towards New Towns for America* (1951) sets out to describe much of his work and contains much practical advice.

STEPHENSON, Gordon, 1908–
Although Stephenson is little known to the public at large he is a widely respected figure in architectural and planning circles both in Britain and abroad.

His career has been as diverse as his influence has been diffuse. Consultant Architect and then Dean at the University of Western Australia since 1960, he is perhaps best remembered in Britain for the intangible yet definite influence he exerted while holding a number of teaching appointments—at Liverpool University where, as lecturer in the School of Architecture (1932–6) under Reilly (q.v.), he was able to introduce his students to the ideas of Le Corbusier (q.v.) in whose office he had recently worked; at the Architectural Association (1939–40); and at Liverpool once more, as Professor of Civic Design (1948–53). Between these two last appointments Stephenson worked for the Government, first as Divisional Architect on Royal Ordnance Factory Work, and later as Research Officer and then Chief Planning Officer at the newly-formed Ministry of Town and Country Planning where he succeeded Holford (q.v.) as head of the Planning Technique Office which prepared a comprehensive programme of planning studies and advisory handbooks. Only one of the handbooks—on Central Area redevelopment—was to materialise but it described methods of carrying out surveys and preparing development plans (q.v.) that were to be invaluable to local authorities for many years to come. While in the civil service Stephenson was also seconded to help Abercrombie (q.v.) on the Greater

London Plan (1943–4), and became a member of the group, led by Lord Reith, that was evolving a national planning policy in the context of the post-war situation.

Stephenson has held a number of appointments abroad. In Western Australia he prepared a Regional Plan for the State Town Planning Commissioner (1954) and he was Professor of Town and Regional Planning at the University of Toronto, Canada (1955–1960).

His published works are:

Community Centres (with Flora Stephenson) (1941).

Planning for Reconstruction (with F. R. S. Yorke) (1944).

Plan for the Metropolitan Region of Perth and Fremantle (with J. A. Hepburn) (1955).

Redevelopment Study of Halifax, Nova Scotia (1957).

A Planning Study of Kingston, Ontario (with G. G. Muirhead) (1959).

STOCKHOLM, Vällingby

Situated nine miles west of Stockholm, Vällingby is the most famous of its several modern suburbs built as part of the city's renowned and carefully planned policy of expansion and decentralization.

Perhaps the term 'satellite' (q.v.) or 'town sector' would be more appropriate, for Vällingby has features not often associated with the conventional suburb. Specifically in order to prevent it becoming a mere dormitory to the city, it was designed to provide employment opportunities for up to 25 per cent of its population (23,000) and, in addition, to serve as a shopping, business and cultural centre for another 60.000 people living nearby in Hässelby and Blackeberg. These areas are linked to it and to the centre of Stockholm by a rapid transit railway system and main roads. With its own suburbs it will eventually have a population of 100,000.

The centre of Vällingby, designed by Backström and Reinius, is a traffic-free precinct (q.v.) built astride the railway and over service roads. It is served by a peripheral car park. Although it lacks any one focal point, the details have been carefully considered. Sprightly lamp posts, fountains, cavorting neon signs and a floorscape of coloured granite setts arranged in wide circles, create a festive and animated atmosphere. Ten- and twelve-storey blocks of flats placed around the centre concentrate a large number of people conveniently near the station and the shops and help to maintain this liveliness after business hours. Visible in many views, they also act as a visual signpost to the centre.

Other residential accommodation, in terraces, cottages and flats is grouped in neighbourhoods of 2,000 to 3,000 people. Existing trees have been carefully preserved and footpaths cross roads by underpass or bridge.

Like the other suburbs of Farsta, Arsta and Grindstorp, Vällingby is widely considered to be a testament to the imaginative and farsighted land policy of Stockholm city. Since 1904, and in anticipation of the rapid growth of population that has indeed occurred, the municipal authority has continued a policy of progressive land acquisition. Until the land acquired has been needed for development it has been used as public recreation areas which in some cases, as at Vällingby, have then been linked with the new development. The development has been related to extension of the railway network.

Vällingby was started in 1953, seven years after the British New Towns Act (q.v.), and there can be little doubt that the Swedes profited from Britain's early experience. The designs of the residential 'superblocks' at Vällingby are generally considered to be more advanced than the layouts at Stevenage, Crawley, or Harlow. Similarly, British architects and planners have been considerably influenced by the Vällingby achievement.

FURTHER READING

Kidder Smith, G. E. (1962). *The New Architecture of Europe.*

Mumford, L. (1961). *The City in History.*

Merlin, Pierre (1971). *New Towns.*

STREET FURNITURE

The term generally used to describe such things as railings, lamp posts, litter-bins, seats, signs, bollards and the many other separate, free-standing items in any street scene.

FURTHER READING
Council of Industrial Design (1970). *Street Furniture from Design Index 1970/71.*

STREET IMPROVEMENT SCHEME
In 1958 the Civic Trust (q.v.) pioneered the Street Improvement Scheme at Magdalen Street, Norwich. Street Improvement Schemes involve the collective re-decoration of property, the removal of unnecessary clutter and the re-placement of ill-designed or confusing signs, poor lighting and street furniture (q.v.). The result can be a striking emergence or re-emergence of a hitherto undistinguished street as one of considerable charm.

The management of such a scheme is by no means easy. It involves establishing a repre-sentative committee to speak for the occupants and co-ordinate plans, engaging an architect to submit an overall scheme and agreeing the con-tractor or contractors to carry out the work. There has to be some check too to ensure that work completed is paid for!

The Civic Trust has a detailed pamphlet that describes the ideal way of promoting and managing such a scheme.

FURTHER READING
Civic Trust (1967). *Street Improvement Schemes. Practice. Notes for Co-ordinating Architects.*

STRUCTURE PLANS
These constitute one part of the Development Plan that each Local Planning Authority is expected to prepare. (The other part is the Local Plan (q.v.).) The Structure Plan consists of a written statement (q.v.) and diagrammatic plans, and deals with main policy and strategic issues. These will have regional implications and must be assessed within a national frame-work. They have to be submitted for approval by the Secretary of State for the Environment.

Structure Plans will normally cover large areas, rural or urban.

FURTHER READING
Ministry of Housing and Local Government (1970). *Development Plans.*
Ministry of Housing and Local Government (1965). *The Future of Development Plans.*

'SUBTOPIA'
A word invented by Ian Nairn in an issue of the *Architectural Review* of 1955 called 'Out-rage'. The article probably did more than any other single factor to reawaken in Britain a concern for environment generally. The word subtopia as Nairn used it, meant 'the world of universal low density mass . . . an even spread of abandoned aerodromes and fake rusticity, wire fences, traffic roundabouts, gratuitous notice boards, car parks and Things-in-Fields.' Nairn saw this extending out from suburbia to the country and back into the devitalised heart of towns, so that the most sublime back-grounds, urban or rural, English or foreign, would soon be seen only over a foreground of casual and unconsidered equipment, litter and lettered admonition.

FURTHER READING
Brett, Lionel (1965). *Landscape in Distress.*
Nairn, Ian (1955). *Outrage.*
Nairn, Ian (1957). *Counter Attack.*

SUPER-ELEVATION
The tilting of a carriageway on a bend to allow high speeds to be maintained by counteracting centrifugal force.

FURTHER READING
Jones, J. H. (1961). *The Geometric Design of Highways.*

T

T.C.P.A. (*see* Town and Country Planning Association).

TEL-EL-AMARNA (14th cent B.C.)

A model village built for workmen employed in building the Egyptian royal city of Akhenaken, which is of much less historical interest. The compact plan of the village displays a true regard for the importance of functional effectiveness. It was a square walled enclosure filled with rows of small houses divided by narrow streets. Each dwelling had a kitchen/sitting room in the front and a bedroom at the rear. Probably planned to ensure discipline, control and good health, it provided, for its time a very human form of environment.

FURTHER READING
Hiorns, Frederick (1956). *Town Building in History.*
Mumford, Lewis (1961). *The City in History.*

TENNESSEE VALLEY AUTHORITY (T.V.A.)

T.V.A. has been rightly called an 'adventure in planning'. It was the first major piece of regional planning on a truly large scale attempted in the United States. Initiated in 1933 as a democratic experiment under the Tennessee Valley Authority Act of that year, a Board was set up to make 'studies, experiments and demonstrations' to promote the use of electric power for agricultural, domestic and industrial purposes. The organisation within T.V.A. consisted of five main divisions under a Board of Directors: Management Service Council; Water Control in the River Channel; Power; Water Control on the Land, and Regional Planning Council. The area of the T.V.A. covered 42,000 square miles (cf. the land area of England, 50,051 sq. miles).

Despite the energy and resources that were injected into the scheme and its obvious relevance to many of the regions of the world, it may be said to have failed to stimulate echoes or copies elsewhere. For whatever reason, and it may be just historical accident, it remains a fairly isolated example of the merits of planning and developing resources on a truly large scale. It seems unlikely, however, that with the re-emergence of interest in the merits of regional planning its achievements will be ignored indefinitely.

FURTHER READING
Liliendhal, David E. (1944). *Democracy on the March.*

TOKYO BAY

Although Japan has no town planning tradition (or perhaps because of it), the *Plan for Tokyo 1960* published by the leading Japanese architect Kenzo Tange is one of the boldest and most unorthodox schemes for city decongestion yet proposed.

With a population of 15 million (1960), Tokyo is the largest and most dense city in the world and still expanding rapidly. An increase of almost 67 per cent is estimated by 1980 and a further 40 per cent by the turn of the century. The unorthodoxy of Tange's proposal lies in its welcoming acceptance of this forecast and its belief that the concentrated growth of cities should not be restricted. In the closely reasoned document which accompanies the illustration of his proposal, Tange argues that the building of satellite towns (q.v.) or other methods of dispersal would be escapist half-measures serving only to vitiate the cultural and economic vitality of the city while failing to have any effect on the causes of its growth. Moreover, by maintaining its traditional radial structure, they would merely contribute to its congestion.

People would move further out, but the centre would retain its hold; commuting distances, traffic problems and inconvenience would all increase. Such measures would thus also impair the development of the 'individual transportation . . . system' which Tange considers an essential element in a modern city. The only solution that would permit both unimpeded growth and maximum personal mobility is, he suggests, 'to shift from a radial centripetal system to a system of linear development'. Thus the plan for Tokyo is neither a proposal for a complete new city nor a policy for de-centralisation. As its subtitle 'Toward A Structural Reorganisation' suggests, it seeks to rehabilitate the existing city and to determine the direction in which future concentrated and dense extensions should take place.

The direction proposed is out over the water of Tokyo Bay where, despite high cost, there would be fewer problems of land acquisition, less disruption of the existing city and less risk of land speculation than with any extension inland. The first stage, in a proposed sequence of four five-year plans, would be the construction of two parallel and interconnected elevated expressways over the buildings in the existing city centre. These would connect with the existing road system at ground level and then be extended across the bay on suspension bridges 131 feet above sea level on each side of a central civic axis containing governmental, commercial and recreational buildings. They would eventually extend to the other side of the bay and would allow a flow of 200,000 cars an hour. An additional 5 to 6 million people could commute to the civic axis by monorail. Off this spine, and connected to it by access roads, some 2 to 2·5 million people would be accommodated in housing units sited on reclaimed land or seeming to float on the water on piers rising from the seabed. On the Tokyo side of the bay an international airport on one side of the axis would be linked to a central station by underground railway. Industrial areas placed on the shores of the bay would be connected to the axis by underwater roads. Once the new linear centre had been established in the bay the old could be rehabilitated.

The proposed buildings take two principal forms. For the civic axis, where it would be essential to keep seabed foundations to a minimum, Tange envisages ten or twenty storey office blocks suspended a hundred or more feet above sea level between load-bearing towers carrying services and elevators. The towers would be placed about 200 feet apart while the office blocks would be different heights and pass over and under each other. Some would curve sinuously above and below the expressways. Growing out from the central axis, the residential units, each $2\frac{1}{2}$ acres square and housing 100,000 people, would consist of enormous tent-like structures recalling the traditional Japanese roofshape. People would build their own homes on platforms built into the curving outer walls. The space between would be occupied by communal facilities and multi-level parking space for 40,000 cars.

The plan was published in magazines and circulated privately in book-form in 1961. Providing an interesting and compelling subject for discussion it is almost certainly too expensive and complex to be implemented.

FURTHER READING
Boyd, Robin (1962). *Kenzo Tange*.

TOWN AND COUNTRY PLANNING ASSOCIATION (T.C.P.A.)

A private organisation open to anyone (or organisation) sympathetic to its aims of securing 'a national policy of landuse planning that will improve living and working conditions, advance industrial and business efficiency, safeguard green belts and the best farm land, and enhance natural, architectural and cultural amenities; so administered as to leave the maximum freedom to private and local initiative consistent with those aims'.

The Association concentrates its resources on spreading a wider understanding of planning principles and ideas and only rarely gets involved in individual battles. Its monthly magazine *Town and Country Planning* is widely read and its weekly *Planning Bulletin* (a digest of cuttings from papers and magazines and a 'new publications' list) is a useful source of information. Founded in 1918 T.C.P.A. was originally called the Garden Cities Association (*see also* Howard, Ebenezer).

ADDRESS
Town and Country Planning Association,
17, Carlton House Terrace, London
SW1Y 5AW

TOWN DEVELOPMENT
The Town Development Act 1952 makes provision for the relief of congestion in large industrial towns in England and Wales (such as London and Birmingham), by encouraging the transfer of population from these areas to places suitable for expansion where employment is provided. Schemes have been approved for providing some 130,000 dwellings in this way, of which about 40,000 have been completed or are in course of construction. Most examples are already well established towns in the South of England and include Basingstoke, Andover, Haverhill.

FURTHER READING
Cullingworth, J. B. (3rd Ed. 1970). *Town and Country Planning in England and Wales.*
Seeley, Ivor H. (1968). *Planned Expansion of Country Towns.*

TOWN MAP
A detailed landuse plan (usually at 6″ to mile but sometimes 4″ to 1 mile) indicating broad zoning. It showed different types of information and its precision was often more apparent than real. It allocated some areas for predominant uses (such as residential and industrial) within which other uses might or might not be permitted. It defined some sites exclusively for single uses and for others recorded ownership rather than the purpose for which they were to be used. For a time some long-term proposals, for which no exact location had been fixed, were indicated by symbols, but this proved so misleading it had to be dropped. Principal roads were shown diagrammatically besides precisely defined sites thus often distorting their boundaries. It was something of a hybrid. Surrounded by formal and centralised procedures which made amendment and up-dating very laborious, it soon became obvious that it failed to meet the complex and changing problems of planning large urban areas and in the 1968 Town and Country Planning Act was superseded by Structure Plans.

FURTHER READING
Ministry of Housing and Local Government (1965). *The Future of Development Plans.*
Ministry of Housing and Local Government (1970). *Development Plans.*

TOWNSCAPE
A word that has become common in the last two decades to describe the total urban scene. It is to the town what landscape is to the country. Although still neglected by many professional planners (q.v.) as a proper objective, good townscape is seemingly understood and appreciated by many laymen. It is this quality of good townscape in historic towns that gives them such wide appeal.

Gorden Cullen, to whom much of the credit is due for focusing professional attention on townscape, describes the creation of townscape as 'the art of relationship'. He says: 'Its purpose is to take all the elements that go to create the environment: buildings, trees, nature, water, traffic, advertisements and so on, and to weave them together in such a way that drama is released.'

It is unfortunate, even if understandable, that people should have come to expect to find good townscape only in old towns and it is a misconception of the term to apply it only to 'good' environment. Townscape exists in all urban areas.

FURTHER READING
Crosby, Theo (1956). *Architecture: City Sense.*
Cullen, Gordon (1961). *Townscape.*
Sharp, Thomas (1968). *Town and Townscape.*
Worskett, Roy (1969). *The Character of Towns.*

TOWN SCHEME
A scheme operated by the Historic Buildings Council (q.v.) in which grant aid is given jointly by government and a local authority

52. Traffic Management: Closed Circuit TV on M4

over a number of years for the preservation of buildings which have architectural or historic significance as groups. In each scheme the Council contributes 25 per cent of the annual costs up to a fixed maximum, the local authority contributes 25 per cent and the owners pay 50 per cent. In the twenty schemes now being operated the annual government grant varies between £2,000 and £10,000. (This excludes the grant of £20,000 for the Bath scheme which was a forerunner of the system and is regarded as a special case.) The initiative must come from a local authority.

FURTHER READING
Historic Buildings Council. (1953–) *Annual Reports.*

TRAFFIC MANAGEMENT
The organisation of a more efficient movement

108

of traffic within a given street system by re-arranging the flows, controlling the intersections and regulating the times and places for parking.

FURTHER READING
Ministry of Transport (1963). *Traffic in Towns* (Buchanan Report).

TRAFFIC SEGREGATION
A term used to describe the idea of separating different types of traffic. Most commonly used with reference to pedestrians and vehicles.

Segregation is achieved in one of two ways:

(i) By so arranging the pattern of vehicle roads and pedestrian ways that they never cross (see Radburn). Stevenage New Town uses this principle in its town centre.

(ii) By physical separation. In its simplest form this is the underpass. More complex schemes may involve the lifting of a whole

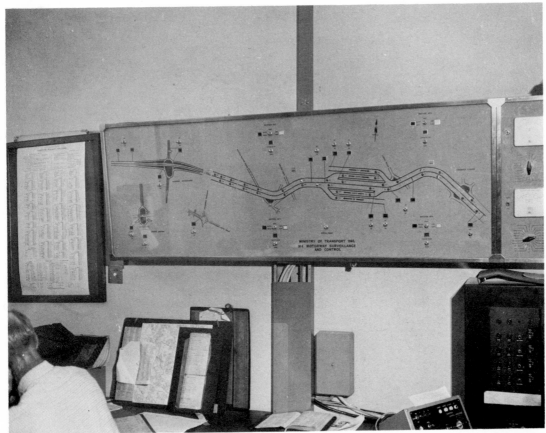

53. Traffic Management: Mimic Diagram in Police
Control Point

central area some 20 feet into the air. (See
Hook and Cumbernauld.)

FURTHER READING
Ministry of Transport (1963). *Traffic in Towns*
  (Buchanan Report).

TRANSPORT (Public, Private, Service)
(a) Public Transport: the umbrella term used
to describe the means of transporting people
(and some goods) to and from their homes to
work or recreation. It covers bus services,
trains and undergrounds. It does not normally
include taxis or coaches and its distinguishing
characteristic is that it runs on predetermined
routes and to a timed schedule.
(b) Private Transport usually describes the
private passenger vehicle: the car owned or
hired by the individual to make numerous,
varied and unscheduled journeys for his own
private purposes. Taxis, privately hired coaches
or vans fall between this and (c) below.
(c) Service. The term is generally used to
describe motor traffic of an industrial or commercial nature generated by the delivery of raw
materials or goods.
N.B. Under the Transport Act 1969 the hours
of work of any one driving a road vehicle for
hire either as private, public or service transport
are severely restricted.

FURTHER READING
Ministry of Transport (1963). *Traffic in Towns*
  (Buchanan Report).

TREE PRESERVATION ORDER
The 1962 Town and Country Planning Act
and the Civic Amenities Act 1967 make provision for the preservation of trees, groups of
trees or woodlands by means of Tree Preservation Orders. These are made by local planning

authorities and confirmed by the Minister of Housing and Local Government. Such orders may be made in the 'interests of amenity'— and these are the only relevant factors.

When in force a T.P.O. prohibits the felling, lopping or wilful destruction of trees except with the consent of the local planning authority. Refusal of consent or limiting by conditions may make the Local Authority liable to pay compensation. In appropriate circumstances the Local Planning Authority may be served with a notice to purchase.

The maximum fine for cutting down or wilfully destroying a tree subject to a T.P.O. is £250 or twice the value of the tree whichever is the greater. The fine relates to each tree covered by the Order.

It is now possible for a local planning authority to make an 'instant' Tree Preservation Order which is fully effective from the moment it is made. Like the machinery for Building Preservation Notices (q.v.), it is designed to help the local authority faced with an urgent situation when speedy action is needed to save a tree from destruction. Such an order is effective from the moment the landowner, on whose land the tree stands, has been notified and remains so for six months, during which time the Minister may confirm or quash the Order or vary its terms.

Two new aspects of tree preservation have emerged with the Civic Amenities Act 1967. A local planning authority is now charged to make such Tree Preservation Orders as seem appropriate in granting permission for any development, and it enables the authority to make a T.P.O. to apply to trees to be planted in accordance with the planning permission. Also, when a tree, protected by a T.P.O. is removed, destroyed or dies it is the owner's duty to replace it with a similar tree which automatically becomes the subject of a Tree Preservation Order.

FURTHER READING
Civic Trust (1967). *The Preservation and Planting of Trees.*

TRUMPET
A two-level version of a T-junction, allowing complete freedom of manoeuvre of all traffic

54. Trumpet

in any direction. The name derived from the resulting shape on plan.

FURTHER READING
Drake, James (1969). *Motorways.*
Jones, J. H. (1961). *The Geometric Design of Modern Highways.*

TWILIGHT ZONE
Around the central area of any large town or city there is usually a ring of older property which is rapidly decaying. The cause of such decay is partly physical and partly social. It usually consists of housing a century or more in age which is now used for light industrial purposes, or is subject to multiple occupancy,

110

being too large for modern (servantless) family life. Maintenance is poor and public utility services are often decaying too. Redevelopment in central areas drives out the poorer businesses into those premises where rents are low and their arrival signals a further process of decay.

Occasionally under extreme pressure for housing near the centre these areas are salvaged by business and professional classes who spend vast sums of money on their repair and, in the process of restoring the fabric, also restore the environment and social qualities. This has happened in parts of London, such as Chelsea, Canonbury and Notting Hill.

FURTHER READING
Keeble, Lewis (4th Ed. 1969). *Principles and Practice of Town and Country Planning.*
Medhurst, Franklin and Parry-Lewis, J. (1969). *Urban Decay.*
Twilight Areas. A Dialogue in March 1969 edition of Official Architecture and Planning.

U

UNWIN, Raymond, 1863–1940

Architect, planner, engineer and writer who has been called 'the father of British town planning'.

Unwin's career as architect and planner divides broadly into two distinct parts. In the first, during his partnership with Barry Parker (q.v.) from 1896 to 1914, he designed New Earswick near York, Letchworth (q.v.) and Hampstead Garden Suburb (q.v.) which, with their culs-de-sac, closes, quadrangles and superblocks, their abundant greenery, substantial private gardens and low density (q.v.), were conspicuously looser in layout than almost any previous urban housing developments and reflected Unwin's belief that the various nineteenth century building and sanitary regulations could not in themselves provide surroundings that would satisfy 'the natural aesthetic hunger of mankind' in which he believed. This was also the period of his three books, *The Art of Building a Home* (with Barry Parker) 1901, *Town Planning in Practice* (1909) and *Nothing Gained by Overcrowding* (1912) in which he first evolved some of his planning ideas, and moved towards formulating the famous and influential Parker and Unwin slogan 'twelve to the acre'.

In the second part, when he worked as chief architect and planner in a number of ministries, Unwin was able to use the experience, authority and lessons gained from his early experiments to influence the direction of national planning policy. Probably his most substantial contributions were to the report of the Tudor Walters Committee on working class housing layouts and the subsequent Ministry of Housing *Manual* (1918), both of which had a far-reaching influence on the design of local authority housing schemes over the next twenty years. They also led Unwin to serve on numerous local government committees.

On his retirement from the civil service in 1928 Unwin became technical adviser to the Greater London Regional Town Planning Committee (1929–33), toured the U.S.A. to report on low cost housing, and was appointed visiting Professor at Columbia University in 1936. He was President of the International Federation for Housing and Town Planning (1928–33) following the death of Sir Ebenezer Howard (q.v.), President of the Royal Institute of British Architects (q.v.) (1931–3), Chairman of the British Building Research Board (1933–4) and R.I.B.A. Gold Medallist in 1937. He was knighted in 1932.

Underlying all Unwin's achievements and writings are the political convictions he formed while a young man working in the industrial towns of the north, where as a member of the Fabian Society and the Ancoats Brotherhood, he preached in the northern labour churches, and was greatly influenced by the writings of

Ruskin and of his friends William Morris and Edward Carpenter.

Town Planning in Practice has been translated into French, German and Russian and is a classic of its time.

FURTHER READING
Bell, Colin and Rose (1969). *City Fathers.*
Creese, W. J. (1966). *The Search for Environment. (The Garden City Before and After).*
Creese, W. J. (1967). *The Legacy of Raymond Unwin (A Human Pattern for Planning).*

UR OF THE CHALDEES
A Sumerian city which probably reached its ultimate size and shape about 2300 B.C. Famous as the earlier home of Abraham, it was excavated in the 1920s by Sir Leonard Woolley and found to have some fascinating characteristics. Half way between Babylon and the Persian Gulf, it had a canal from the Euphrates to the docks at the city boundary.

Well raised above the general level was the Teminos, a religious area that is regarded by many experts as the forerunner of the Acropolis that was to be a notable part of many cities in later times. Of almost equal interest is the evidence that Ur had a residential area containing well ordered streets of two-storey houses built around courtyards with proper drainage systems and facilities for washing.

FURTHER READING
Hiorns, Frederick (1956). *Town Building in History.*
Mumford, Lewis (1961). *The City in History.*
Woolley, Leonard (2nd Ed. Reprint 1950). *Ur of the Chaldees.*

URBAN RENEWAL
A general term to describe the idea of consciously renewing the outworn areas of towns and cities. Over the years the meaning has become blurred and now covers most aspects of renewal, including both re-development and re-habilitation. But still, in this country, major urban renewal schemes have been largely concerned with demolition and re-development, whereas in America the phrase refers more specifically to schemes of re-furnishing existing property. (See Rehabilitation and Environmental Recovery.)

In the early 1950s when the idea of renewal was not generally accepted and planning thought tended to be more concentrated on New Towns, a Society for the Promotion of Urban Renewal (S.P.U.R.) (q.v.) was formed with a great many well-known planners in its membership.

FURTHER READING
Johnson-Marshall. Percy (1966). *Rebuilding Cities.*
Civic Trust for the North West (1969). *Environmental Recovery at Skelmersdale.*

USE CLASSES ORDER
This order prescribes classes of use within which certain changes may take place without development (q.v.) occurring and therefore no question of planning permission arising. The order divides uses up into classes and change from one class to another is not allowed without permission from the Local Planning Authority. The order is also careful to ensure that some uses, which would otherwise fall within a particular class, are specifically excluded. For example fried fish shops, tripe shops, pet shops and cats meat shops are excluded from Class 1 which is for shops. Consequently to change a tobacconist's shop into a shoe shop does not constitute development but to change a bookshop into a tripe shop does.

FURTHER READING
Cullingworth, J. B. (3rd Ed. 1970). *Town and Country Planning in England and Wales.*
Heap, Desmond (5th Ed. 1969). *An Outline of Planning Law.*

UTHWATT COMMITTEE ON COMPENSATION AND BETTERMENT
A committee set up in 1941 (along with the Beveridge Committee on Social Insurance and Allied Services and the Scott Committee on

opposite
55. Urban Renewal: After slum clearance in Hulme, Manchester

Land Utilisation in Rural Areas (q.v.)) to consider one aspect of the problems of postwar reconstruction. It was this committee's task to devise a scheme which would make possible 'the resolution of competing claims and the allocation of land for the various requirements . . . on the basis of selecting the most suitable land for the particular purpose, irrespective of the existing values which may attach to the individual parcels of land'. At once they were face to face with the problems that flow from restricting individual freedom and the right of the individual to be compensated for financial loss resulting from such restrictions; and, obversely, the best way of 'taxing' him for any 'betterment' that might accrue to him personally from proposals made in the best interests of the whole community.

Faced with this the Uthwatt Committee concluded that a new system of land ownership was necessary, considered nationalisation but rejected it and finally decided that the solution lay in the nationalisation of all development rights in undeveloped land. This, essentially,

was built into the 1947 Town and Country Planning Act. No development could take place without the local planning authority's permission. If permission were refused no compensation (q.v.) would be paid (except in a number of special cases). If granted, any resulting increase in land value was to be subject to a development charge.

In practice the system did not work, was substantially altered and dismantled in 1954 and 1959. During 1966–70 the idea was revived with the Land Commission and development levy but abolished with a change of government in 1970 and the problem of compensation and betterment remains largely unsolved today.

FURTHER READING
Report of the Expert Committee on Compensation and Betterment (Uthwatt Report) cmnd 6386 HMSO 1942.
Cullingworth, J. B. (3rd Ed. 1970). *Town and Country Planning in England and Wales.*

VACANT LAND

A loose term sometimes used to describe derelict land and often, instead, wasteland. Generally taken to mean land, often in small pockets, having no obvious use and in a state of neglect. Such 'wasteland' can, where it is injurious to amenity, be the subject of a notice by the Local Planning Authority to the owner requiring that the matter be rectified. This power has, however, only rarely been used due to the difficulties of defining such injury and the subsequent lengthy procedures of enforcement.

VÄLLINGBY (*see* Stockholm)

THE VICTORIAN SOCIETY

The Victorian Society exists for the study and protection of Victorian and Edwardian architecture and other arts. It was founded by the

Countess of Rosse in 1958 and is a registered charity dependent financially on subscribing members. Regional groups have been formed in Liverpool, Manchester and the West Midlands. The term Victorian is used to cover the period 1830–1914.

ADDRESS
Victorian Society, 12, Magnolia Wharf, Strand-on-the-Green, London, W4.

VITRUVIUS 1st Century B.C.

Is undoubtedly the most famous architect/planner of Antiquity. An Augustan architect, Vitruvius owes his fame not so much to completed works as to his ten books on architecture dating from about 30 to 27 B.C.—*De Architectura.* The book was rediscovered in the

Middle Ages and, being the only treatise to survive from Antiquity, rapidly became the standard reference book on the classical style of building so much admired by the Renaissance mind.

Most of the ten books deal with details of architectural and building technique, but the fourth to the seventh chapters of his first book are concerned generally with town planning and embody fundamental principles for the layout and form of whole towns. Vitruvius approached the problem from the notions of convenience, health and amenity. Illustrating his ideas with a simple diagram he lists the advantages of elevated sites and indicates ways of avoiding fogs, damp, keen winds and excessive heat. The location of streets, buildings and open spaces is considered and he indicates the advantages of certain sites or dispositions for different buildings. The circular town is advocated, with the main internal roads on a radial/concentric principle to facilitate easy access from the perimeter gates to the centre and create well-shaped sites for building. His detailed thinking is indicated by his recommendation that the radial roads should not be centred on the gates, thus avoiding strong winds.

Although medieval builders had evolved the concentric town plan, the Vitruvian concentric/radial plan [13 centuries earlier] was an original idea as no ancient town exhibited these rationalistic principles.

FURTHER READING
Hiorns, Frederick (1956). *Town Building in History.*

WEAVING

The movement of traffic from one lane to another, whilst travelling at moderately fast speeds, in order that they may be in the correct road position for some intended manoeuvre.

FURTHER READING
Davies, Ernest (1960). *Roads and their Traffic.*

WELWYN

The second English Garden City and, like its predecessor at Letchworth (q.v.) an attempt to persuade government to adopt a national policy of planned and ordered dispersal.

Even more than Letchworth, Welwyn owes its existence to the determination and idealism of Ebenezer Howard (q.v.). By 1918 Letchworth had successfully established itself as a self-contained industrial town with a substantial population and had earned an international reputation. But it had found no imitators. Superficial architectural and layout characteristics had been copied in innumerable suburbs and speculative developments erroneously described as 'on garden city lines', but the underlying planning principles seemed to have been forgotten. Frederic Osborn (q.v.) and the Garden Cities and Town Planning Association (now the Town and Country Planning Association (q.v.)) were renewing their propaganda campaign for the garden city concept, but Howard believed that only a second practical demonstration would influence government policy. In 1919 he collected about £5,000 from friends and, without consulting his colleagues, purchased nearly 1,500 acres of land (for £51,000) in Hertfordshire about four miles north of Hatfield. The Welwyn Garden City Company was formed in 1920.

Similar in concept and general character to Letchworth, Welwyn is widely considered to be more successfully compact and urban in layout and to exhibit a higher degree of overall architectural control. The plan and many of the red-brick neo-Georgian houses were designed by Louis de Soissons.

Sir Frederic Osborn, who has been closely involved with the garden city and New Towns (q.v.) movement, has suggested that, but for Welwyn, Letchworth 'might have enjoyed a mere *succès d'estime* and been left on the map as a vestige of an impracticable early-twentieth-century ideal'.

In 1948 following the New Towns Act (q.v.) the management of Welwyn passed to a government development corporation.

FURTHER READING

Osborn, F. J. and Whittick, Arnold (2nd Ed. 1969). *New Towns: The Answer to Megalopolis.*

Ashworth, W. (1954). *The Genesis of Modern British Town Planning.* (1968 latest Ed.)

Creese, Walter J. (1966). *The Search for Environment (The Garden City Before and After).*

Osborn, F. J. (2nd Ed. 1969). *Green Belt Cities.*

WHITE LAND

Land given no particular allocation on a Development Plan (q.v.). Planning permission is required before development may proceed and any type of development may be considered by the Local Planning Authority, in theory. In practice Local Planning Authorities have often treated white land as if it were Green Belt (q.v.) and refused permission, a decision frequently reversed by the Minister on appeal.

FURTHER READING

Cullingworth, J. B. (3rd Ed. 1970). *Town and Country Planning in England and Wales.*

Ministry of Housing and Local Government (1967). *Planning Bulletin 8; Settlement in The Countryside.*

WILLIAMS-ELLIS, Sir Clough, 1883–

Architect, author, propagandist and creator of the village of Portmeirion in Wales.

In its creator's words Portmeirion is an 'unashamedly romantic' collection of buildings of every conceivable shape and style carefully sited amongst trees, bushes, exotic flowers and terraced gardens on the slopes of a hill overlooking the Welsh coast. Incorporating relics and facades retrieved from demolished buildings, interspersed with columns, spires and pinnacles and crowned with a 'stately pleasure dome', it is lighthearted, extravagant and fanciful in spirit but not without serious intent; it was conceived partly as an antidote to the often dull functionalism of modern architecture, partly as an attempt to win 'as yet uninterested and uninformed popular support for architecture, planning, landscaping, the use of colour and indeed for design generally ...'.

As such it is merely one manifestation, if perhaps the best known, of Williams-Ellis' crusading efforts to awaken public concern for amenity and seemliness in the environment. His *England and the Octopus* published in 1928, was one of the first books to warn of the ugliness and consequences of continuing urban sprawl, while his *Pleasures of Architecture* (written with his wife) probably awoke in many people their first interest in architecture. Under his presidency the Design and Industries Association published a series of illustrated and scathing 'Cautionary Guides' to all that seemed inelegant and visually squalid in a number of towns (among them Oxford, Carlisle and St Alban's), thus stimulating the growth of a number of local amenity societies (q.v.). The creation of the Snowdonia National Park (q.v.) in 1951 was partly due to his earlier acquisition and presentation to the National Trust (q.v.) of some of the land.

Williams-Ellis was the first Chairman of the first New Town Development Corporation at Stevenage and he is Vice-President of the Council for the Protection of Rural Wales and of the Institute of Landscape Architects. Williams-Ellis was knighted in the New Year's Honours List 1972. In addition to the works mentioned, his principal publications are:

Reconnography.
Cottage Building.
Building in Pise.
The Architect.
Face of the Land (edited).
Britain and the Beast (edited).
Town and Country Planning.
The Adventure of Building.

Architecture Here & Now (with Sir John
  Summerson).
Protection of Ancient Buildings.
Plan for Living.
On Trust to the Nation.
Portmeirion.
The Place & its Meaning.
Roads in the Landscape.
Architect Errant (autobiography).

WRITTEN STATEMENT

Under the 1947 Town and Country Planning
Act, a printed document to accompany a town
or country map, describing the general policy
and intentions of the local planning authority.
Together with the appropriate map it constitutes the Development Plan (q.v.) which when
approved by the Minister, has the force of
law. It usually contains references to zoning.
density, programming, open space, education
facilities and any special provisions contained in the plan.

Under the 1968 Town and Country Planning Act it has even greater significance as the
document accompanying a Structure Plan
(q.v.) which being much more diagrammatic,
needs a correspondingly more precise statement
of objectives.

FURTHER READING
Keeble, Lewis (4th Ed. 1969). *Principles and
Practice of Town and Country Planning.*

APPENDIX

Stevenage, Hertfordshire was the first of the new towns. Before the 1946 Act it was one of the satellite towns proposed by Abercrombie in the Greater London plan. 6,100 acres, approx. 30 miles from central London. Pop. proposed 60,000 in neighbourhood units of up to 10,000. This was later increased to 105,000.

Crawley, Sussex was designated as a new town area in January 1947. Lies 30 miles from London. Planned originally to have a population of 50,000 but will now extend to 80,000 by 1981. Its eleven neighbourhoods were planned around a town centre with an industrial zone to the north of the site.

Hemel Hempstead, Hertfordshire. This existing town of 21,000 people was designated as a new town in February 1947 with an expected population of 80,000. The site of 5,910 acres is approximately 25 miles from London. The new town was grafted on the existing old town which now occupies the central area in the expanded plan.

Harlow, Essex was another of the Abercrombie satellite town sites for Greater London and was designated as a new town in March 1947. The site covers 6,400 acres and is 23 miles from London. The master plan was prepared by Frederick Gibberd and submitted in 1949. Originally planned as a 90,000 population town it has now been increased to 125,000. The net density for housing amounts to 50 persons per acre. The plan is divided up into four main areas all of which fit into a roughly rectangularly shaped site.

Welwyn Garden City, Hertfordshire was the second pioneer garden city built according to the proposals outlined by Ebenezer Howard in 1919–20. Letchworth had been built earlier in 1904–6. It was originally intended to have a population of 60,000 but had reached less than 20,000 by 1948. In that year it was designated a new town and a corporation was set up to develop it and the neighbouring new town Hatfield. For the new town of Welwyn a population of 36,500 was envisaged but this was increased to 50,000 in 1954.

Hatfield, Hertfordshire is one of the smaller new towns with an area of 2,350 acres and a maximum population of 29,000. It lies approximately 18 miles from London and $2\frac{1}{2}$ miles from its neighbour Welwyn Garden City. The master plan for Hatfield was prepared by Lionel Brett who has also been responsible for a number of the houses which are disposed in seven neighbourhoods on the north and south sides of the new town centre.

Basildon, Essex is a new town centred on two existing towns, Laindon and Pitsea. The town was designated, with a site of 7,818 acres, in 1949. The town will eventually have a population of 133,000, and serve the needs of the surrounding districts with its additional 45,000 people. The plan is divided into ten neighbourhoods and the large town centre is pedestrianised.

Bracknell, Berkshire was designated in 1949 and was originally intended for a population of 25,000. This has been increased to a maximum growth of 60,000. The site is 30 miles from London and 10 miles from Reading.

Six other new towns built in England and Wales were designed to serve the special needs of their areas, *Newton Aycliffe* (1947) and *Peterlee* (1948) at Durham, *Corby* (1950) in Northamptonshire, and *Cwmbran* (1949), Monmouthshire. The new towns of *Skelmersdale* (1961), Lancs., and *Runcorn* (1964), Cheshire, are to meet the overspill needs of Merseyside while *Dawley* (1963) Shropshire, and *Redditch* (1964) meet those of Birmingham. In 1968 Dawley was enlarged by the inclusion of Wellington and Oakengates and renamed Telford. Central Lancashire (1970) and Milton Keynes (1967) are for 500,000 and 250,000 respectively. The Scottish new towns consist of: *Cumbernauld* (1955), Dunbartonshire, which has caused considerable interest through the design of its town centre; *East Kilbride* (1947), Lanarkshire; *Glenrothes* (1948), Fife; *Livingston* (1962), West Lothian, all of which serve the excess population problems of Glasgow.

INDEX